THE POWER OF COMMUNITY AT THE OHIO STATE UNIVERSITY

MASTER TEAGUE III

THE POWER OF COMMUNITY AT THE OHIO STATE UNIVERSITY

SHINE GOD'S LIGHT
MAKE KINGDOM IMPACT

Published by Master W. Teague III

CONTENTS

CONTENTS

ACKNOWLEDGEMENTS

Firstly, I want to acknowledge the Great I Am who is the Lord God Almighty. There is no stability, purpose, or meaning to life without Him.

I would be remiss if I did not acknowledge all athletes, coaches, students and faculty of The Ohio State University who faithfully stood for Christ. There has been many known and unknown names throughout the history of OSU that paved the way for the next generation of Christ followers to have impact and stand bold in the truth. For that, I am very grateful. I am just one small piece in the wholistic plan of God to make His kingdom come and His will be done.

I also want to acknowledge and thank all my brothers, sisters, and elders in Christ that helped me make this book what it is and allowed me to share their impact on my life. I want to specifically thank Pastor Doyle Jackson and his wife Jennifer Jackson for encouraging me to write this book. It took several months for me to put pin to paper as I needed to gain faith and courage that I could do it. After thought and prayer, the Holy Spirit moved me to write until it was finished. Now, I want to acknowledge every person that will read this and say, thank you. I pray that this book speaks to you and blesses you the way it is supposed to and that would be to the credit of the Lord and not myself. Enjoy and God bless!

FORMER OSU PLAYERS & COACHES OF IMPACT

FROM 1990 AND ON:

NOTABLE PLAYERS
(THIS IS NOT AN EXHAUSTIVE LIST OF PLAYERS)

KENT GRAHAM (QB)

TAYLER GRAHAM (QB)

BUTLER B'YNOTE' (RB)

LUKE FICKELL (DE)

JOHN PETERSON (OL)

OBIE STILLWELL (LB)

AHMED PLUMMER (CB)

MIKE DOSS (DB)

BEN HARTSOCK (TE)

DUSTIN FOX (DB)

ANTHONY SCHLEGEL (LB)

JASON CALDWELL (TE)

JOEL PENTON (DL)

ANTONIO SMITH (DB)

CRAIG KRENZEL (QB)

MAURICE HALL (RB)

JOE GANTZ (RB)

MALCOM JENKINS (DB)

MARCUS FREEMAN (LB)

DOUG WORTHINGTON (DL)

STAN WHITE JR (RB)

JIM CORDLE (OL)

CAMERON HEYWARD (DL)

KENNY GUITON (QB)

RYAN SHAZIER (LB)

JT BARRETT (QB)

SHAUN WADE (DB)

JOSH MYERS (OL)

KAM BABB (WR)

CJ STROUD (QB)

JUSTIN FIELDS (QB)

NOTABLE COAHCES
(THIS IS NOT AN EXHAUSTIVE LIST OF COACHES)

JIM TRESSEL

MARK DANTONIO

LUKE FICKELL

LARRY JOHNSON

JAMES LAURINAITIS

KENNY PARKER

QUINN BARHAM

PHIL MATUSZ

NIKO PALAZETI

CHRIS FENELON

(NO ONE ON THESE LISTS ARE PERFECT AND ARE NOT EXPECTED TO BE PERFECT | ALTHOUGH THESE INDIVIDUALS PLAYED AN INTENTIONAL, PERSONAL, AND IMPACTFUL ROLE IN THE BODY OF CHRIST AT THE OSU)

FOREWORD BY ROY HALL

FORMER OSU FOOTBALLER &
FOUNDER OF THE DRIVEN FOUNDA-
TION

I wanted to take a moment to express my sincere admiration and excitement regarding this book, "The Power Of Community At The Ohio State University | Shine God's Light: Make Kingdom Impact." Master's journey, experiences, and stories that he poured into this book are set to impact not just a few, but thousands of lives.

His commitment and unwavering faith in Jesus shine through in every word he penned. His ability to weave his experiences at The Ohio State University with the greater purpose of shining God's light is truly remarkable. It's evident that this book is not just a collection of stories; it's a testament to the transformative power of a community and faith.

I want to thank him for being obedient to this calling and for allowing the Holy Spirit to guide his words. His dedication to sharing these narratives and insights is a testament to the faith and the love he has for others. This work is a reflection of Proverbs 3:5-6, "Trust in the Lord with all your heart and lean not on your own understanding; in all your ways submit to him, and he will make your paths straight."

As Master embarks on this exciting chapter of his journey, I want to remind him that this is just the beginning. With every calling comes a cost, a willingness to sacrifice more than ever before to ensure that God's word reaches the masses. This book is a beacon of hope and inspiration, and I have no doubt that its impact will far exceed expectations.

I also want to express gratitude for a sneak peek into this book. It truly is an easy read, yet its depth and authenticity will resonate with people of all ages. Master's ability to connect with the readers is a gift, and I believe that many lives will be touched and transformed through the messages shared.

This book is a testament to the obedience, the faith, and the passion for making a difference. May the words in this book bring comfort, encouragement, and enlightenment to those who read them.

This book is a source of inspiration and shares a great light with the world. May this book reach far and wide, touching hearts and sparking change.

With admiration and support,

Roy Hall

A WORD FROM MASTER

Welcome! Before we get into this, I want to share what I hope and pray you get out of this book...

The Barna Group estimates that around 70% of professing Christians that go to college end up walking away from the faith during that time. I believe a large factor in this statistic is the lack of community and connection with other believers. So, I decided to write this book about 'The Power Of Community At The Ohio State University' and encourage you to 'Shine God's Light' and 'Make Kingdom Impact' through sharing my own journey. It is important that believers in Christ are connected with other believers in Christ (the church - not the physical building but the children of God). We are in fact the body of Christ which consist of all those that have entrusted their lives to him in this world. That body is a community, which means communication and working together is essential to flourishing and running properly. Intentionally connecting to that community helps each one of us better use the gifts that God gave us to bless others. Fellowshipping with other children of God help us stand firmer, taller, and shine brighter in the truth. That truth is Christ.

In this book, I first share the beginning of my journey with Christ and a collection of testimonies from my youth. Chapters three through six focus on my college years from 2018 to 2021. I went to The Ohio State University on a football scholarship and arrived on campus at seventeen years old. I want to share how surrounding myself with a community of believers helped me grow my faith and walk with Christ in college and shine God's light in a dark world.

Lastly, in chapter seven I close out by discussing the position and perspective believers in Christ should have. I also encourage us again to be in community and shine God's light through love and good deeds.

I hope to encourage the student athlete and student going to college or already in college that you do not have to follow the crowd. You can in fact stand firm in Christ and make kingdom impact. I want to help parents and guardians better prepare those students for the wiles of college by sharing what helped prepare me. This book also is for the Christ Follower in general as I am encouraging believers everywhere to be in community and shine brighter the light you have been given. And lastly, I created this book for those that may want a glimpse into my college experience and faith journey in hopes to serve you as well.

I pray this book will encourage and inspire you to get in community, be the light God calls you to be, and make Kingdom impact.

EARLY FAITH JOURNEY

My Genesis

I was the tender age of ten when I placed my trust in Jesus Christ and was baptized at my hometown church in Murfreesboro Tennessee. As a boy and teenager, the Holy Spirit worked tremendously through my life. Both my mom and dad were key factors in the start of my journey in walking with the Lord.

In grade school and junior high I saw my dad reading this big book all the time. He read it early in the morning, during the day, and at night. It was always with him, so I knew there was something special about it if he read it this often. I looked up to my dad and I wanted to be just like him. So, it made since that I became curious about this big book he buried his head in. Can you guess what book he was reading? Yes, the Bible. He did his daily morning reading and time with the Lord in our home office. I soon found myself joining him. It was his personal time with the Lord. Nonetheless he allowed me to study with him. This had a profound impact on me and not only my relationship with my dad but my pursuit of God and his Word.

Eventually, I began carrying around my personal Bible and reading it on my own. I even carried it to school every day and read it. I did this in middle school, high school, and college. I am certainly not a Bible genius; I just knew reading the Bible was important. It is in fact where the creator of all things speaks to us. There is not more important words we could read, agreed? Someone may ask, "did taking your Bible to school and reading it ever offend anyone?" To that I would say perhaps, but I do not remember, and if it did, I did not pay attention to it because guess what, the next day I carried it and read it again.

In Joshua 1:8 the Bible says to, *"Keep this Book of the Law always on your lips; meditate on it day and night, so that you may be careful to do everything written in it. Then you will be prosperous and successful."* I did not know it when I first started reading my Bible as a youth, but I now see that I practiced a biblical principle. My classmates occasionally asked me, "what are you reading?" I was most likely reading in the New Testament. I honestly did not read the Old Testament as a youngster besides Genesis, Exodus, Psalms, and Proverbs. I am sure you folks reading this can relate to that. It all just seemed complicated. Although, I can tell you that what I did read, eventually downloaded into my brain. The Holy Spirit reminded me of scripture that I had read, and he quickened my mind and gave me wisdom about what it means to be obedient to the Lord.

I am not saying I was perfect and followed the Spirit's leading at every turn. There were worldly ways and temptations that I dealt with growing up that I had to overcome. With the help of the Holy Spirit, I have overcome many of them and am still overcoming other shortcomings today. In the next pages I will share testimonies of how God continued to do great things in my life growing up.

Youth Retreat

Every summer, my church held a weeklong youth camp. We did fun activities to build faith and courage alongside our peers. Although, you could not go to anymore youth retreats after you passed the sixth grade. These retreats were the best times I had at church. So, when I got to sixth grade, I knew I had to make it count. Fortunately, the church made the sixth-grade retreat special.

We went to an offsite campground where they had obstacle courses, white water rafting, zip-lines, and caves. When it was time for me to go, I was ecstatic, and had grand expectations. When we arrived and settled in, we had worship services, praying sessions, small groups with our camp counselors, compete in challenges, and do all the activities the camp had. The worship services and walking through the caves were my favorite things we did. During those worship services I felt the presence of the Lord like I never have before in my youth. The eyes of the campers, including mine, filled with tears. My view of God became grander and more glorious. We worshiped at night when all the stars were out, and it reminded me of His awesomeness and creativity. Psalms 19:1-2 says, *"The heavens declare the glory of God; the skies proclaim the work of his hands."* How beautiful is that?

Going into the caves was another memorable experience. It was quite fun; I would say it was a frightful adventure. We all had on hard hats with lights on them as it was very dark. Although, it felt like they were too dim to see as clearly as I wanted to. Inside the caves we learned to trust our guide knew the pathway through and back out again. We had to understand that going our own way would mean we would get lost or even worse. This was an example of Jesus being the way the truth and the life. If we do not go the way of Jesus, we will be lost and go our own way. If we do not see Jesus as the truth, the lie will be our guide. If we do not see Jesus as the life, death will be our end. Not only was following our guide the only way we could get out, the corridors and passageways in the cave were tight and narrow to the point that I questioned if I could get through them.

In Matthew 7:13-14 Jesus says, *"wide is the gate and broad is the road that leads to destruction, and many enter through it, but small is the gate and narrow is the road that leads to life, and few find it."*

Going through those caves was a practical way for us to understand that truth. When the camp was over and we drove back home, I gazed out the window at God's creation in awe of Him. This camp was a memorable moment that elevated my faith and respect for God to a new level.

English Class

Let me tell you a story from middle school that my family laughs about to this day. In sixth grade I took an English class taught by a lovely old lady. Although, some would not have called her lovely at all as she was quite strict. I on the other hand did not have a problem with stern teachers.

Anyway, if I recall correctly there was one quarter in the year when she wanted us to read a certain number of books. Well, I had it in my head that I was not going to read those books, and I did not. I justified this decision in my mind by saying, "Why would I need to read any other book than the Bible, that's all I need, so I think I'll pass." Guess what, I got a D in that class for the quarter. My standard and the standard in the household were A's and B's, and I missed it big time. So, I did get a D, but I had a great excuse, right? Yeah, I thought I did at the time, but it was far from it. My parents did not accept that as an excuse, and here is why. Colossians 3:23 says, *"Whatever you do, work at it with all your heart, as for working for the Lord, not for human masters."*

My parents expressed to me that I had a responsibility onto God to do my best in all I did, and that includes English class. Even though I made an excuse, I knew deep down that I should have been listening to my teacher and reading the books she asked me to.

The next quarter, I read my books and my grade improved tremendously, and I met my standard, the standard in my household, and most importantly I honored God by doing my best. This was a lesson I needed to learn, because the real reason was that I just did not like to read. Isn't it ironic that I am authoring this book now? That is surprising! Anyway, I had to understand that sometimes honoring the Lord is hard especially when we do not like the responsibilities we have. That is when we should lean on the Lord the most.

Making A Friend

Early in high school, I formed a friendship with a student named Kyle who was in the grade below me. Kyle was often picked on, left out, and treated as less than. So, I decided to befriend him and show him that he mattered to me. At this point in time, I became a top football player in my state and began accumulating college offers. My peers at school respected and looked up to me. Those same peers were the ones picking on, leaving out, and treating Kyle as less than. So, when I decided to befriend him, it was peculiar. Imagine for a second that you were one of the people that picked on and treated Kyle as less than.

What would you think if someone you respected befriended Kyle and treated him the exact opposite of how you did? It may cause you to rethink why you treat Kyle the way you do and encourage you to change that. This is what happened in this situation. I noticed people did not pick on

Kyle when I was with him. So, when I got the chance to sit with him, I did.

As believers we are called to love God more than anything else and love others as ourselves. Matthew 22:37-39 says, "Jesus replied: *"'Love the Lord your God with all your heart and with all your soul and with all your mind.' This is the first and greatest commandment. And the second is like it: 'Love your neighbor as yourself.'*

It was this love that led me to make friends with Kyle. As I said before, I made a habit of carrying my Bible to school every day and reading it. So, as I befriended him, I would always have my Bible with me. It was natural that we eventually began to have discussions about God and faith. As we built our relationship, I started praying and reading the Bible with him. I did my best to explain God and the scriptures to him. I encouraged him to carry his own Bible to school just like I did. I guess you could say we became Bible friends. I would walk down the hall and see Kyle walking the opposite way, Bible in hand. It was a reminder that we do not follow the crowd.

At the time I did not realize how great that was and how the Holy Spirit used me to affect a peer in that way. My new friend soon entrusted his life to Christ and started going to church. He expressed to me the joy of connecting with the church youth group and his youth pastor. I for sure saw a change in him and the way he spoke and his behavior. I saw that he was more conscious of God and His ways and aligning himself to that. We remained friends through high school and are still friends today. He still reminds me of how much he appreciated me encouraging him in the Lord and to be bold for Christ. Although, I would say it was not me but Christ in me that encouraged and impacted his life.

Fellowship Of Christian Athletes

In middle school and high school, I attended Fellowship of Christian Athletes, most know it as FCA. It is a group where Christian athletes of like mind can be in community and grow together in Christ. These meetings were student athlete led, and our FCA consisted of about 3 to 4 leaders that shared messages every week and prepared other gathering events. Freshman and Sophomore year, I was a faithful attendee and was in community with brothers and sisters in Christ. I also invited several teammates, though with FCA starting at 8am which was 30 minutes before school started, it was hard to get some of the guys there. Though, many of them eventually came and I believe seeds were planted in those guys. During my junior and senior year, I was known as a strong person of faith and a great athlete. So, I became an FCA leader alongside a few other athletes. This helped me step out of my comfort zone and talk in front of my peers about the good Word of God. The other FCA leaders and I alternated each week and shared a message from the scripture. After sharing, we split up into small groups where we would discuss and talk further about the message presented.

Every year our district held an FCA event called 'Night of Impact' where several high school FCA's would have a student representative come and speak on behalf of their school. They would talk about what God has been doing on their campus. My senior year, I was blessed to be chosen for that honor, so I got to share what God was doing at my school. As the event neared, I became quite nervous, as this was my first time talking in front of a large group of people.

Cool side note, while I was there, I met pro football hall of fame wide receiver Raymond Berry and got a signed pigskin football from him, that was very cool.

Anyway, on arriving at the event, we sat down and ate, and after that, the FCA area director made introductory statements. Once introductory statements were complete, all the representatives went up on stage and we each took turns sharing about our specific school's FCA group. My heart began to pump heavier and heavier as the microphone got closer and closer to me. Then, when the microphone hit my hand, my nerves settled, and the Holy Spirit gave me the words to say. When it was over, I was grateful that I got to represent my school and how God was impacting all those involved. It was the beginning of more opportunities I got to share the Lord's work with others.

Sharing God's Goodness

Another opportunity that I got to share my faith and testimony was at a local church high school group. The pastor invited me to be interviewed and share with the group how I kept faith in Christ in life, school, and football. There were well over one hundred people in the room, so guess what, my heart was pumping fast. Like the FCA meeting, once I started to speak, my nerves began to go away. By God's grace the Holy Spirit helped me speak clearly. After the service, I was thankful to the Lord for the opportunity to share His goodness in my life to others.

Many students thanked me for coming and sharing, and many felt that my testimony resonated with them. I not only was able to be a light and encourage others in the Lord, but I was impacted by those that listened and those I spoke with afterwards. My faith in the Lord strengthened through both speaking experiences as I had to lean on the Lord to do something I did not feel qualified to do.

It reminds me of when Jesus said to the apostle Paul in 2 Corinthians 12:9, *"My grace is sufficient for you, my power is made perfect in weakness."*

It was in my weakness that allowed me to do this in the Lord's strength.

The Team Experience

While I was on the football team in high school, many of my teammates did not understand why I did not act and do the same things that they did. These were the teammates that would dare me to do things that were less than holy. There were times when I spoke, and if there was anything that remotely sounded like a curse word, they pinned me for it. They would say, "hey bro, I heard you curse man, don't lie." I would always explain that just because you are not used to someone not cursing does not mean I curse too. On the other hand, some understood and admired my lifestyle to honor the Lord. Some would express their desire to be a Christian or more Christian like, but their desire to please their flesh and follow the world were greater. There were also a handful of teammates who were actively pursuing Christ.

I say this to say that when you are in sports and are a part of a large team, there are many kinds of people with diverse backgrounds, values, and beliefs. Being in an environment like that allowed me to learn how to love and co-exist with a variety of people with different beliefs. Although, I did not just learn to co-exist, I learned how not to compromise my values and be the light God has called me to be. Although I was not perfect, accountability from the Holy Spirit, my family, and my brothers and sisters in Christ, helped me stay more committed to God's ways.

My success on the football field caused my teammates and classmates to be curious about how that success happened and opened the door to many conversations. This was the perfect opportunity for me to share how God is the one who strengthens me to play and be great at it. It is only in Christ that I can compete at a high level because all things, I repeat, all things are made by Him, through Him, and for him (see Colossians 3:16). Rest assured; he can do amazing things through you when you believe that.

An Unknown Impact

In high school I had a teammate named Amir. The first year he and I became teammates, we both played running back and competed for reps and play time. Although, I knew he was much better than I was. As I continued to work on my craft, I began to surpass him and all the other players in my school. I not only surpassed the players in my school but players in the county, state, and nation. So, obviously, I became the starting running back. Fast forward to when I was two years in at OSU and 3 years removed from when I last saw Amir, he reached out to me unexpectedly. When we talked, he shared something with me that I will never forget. What he told me caused me to rejoice and praise God.

He explained how he was on vacation drinking, partying, and having a good time with his friends. While he was driving back, he had an encounter with the Lord that was undeniable and life changing. Brought to his end, he chose to place his faith and surrender his life to Christ because the Holy Spirit showed him that what he was doing would lead nowhere but death. I was surprised by the call from him, but I was joyful to hear this testimony and praised God for it.

He then talked to me about high school football and expressed he was jealous he never got to be the starting running back. He explained that when he came to the program it was his goal to be the starter and see successes like the ones I had. He also said that he thought I was an odd person because He did not understand my faith walk with the Lord and why I took it so seriously. He saw that I was different than most people and that was more of a negative than a positive. Although, as he thought back on high school in hindsight, he felt the reason he came to that high school football program was not to succeed in football the way he thought, but to see the Lord in me. My teammate noted that seeing me remain faithful to the Lord even when it was unpopular had a major impact on him (my faithfulness is only a reflection of God's faithfulness to me).

When I heard this, I was surprised that he was paying attention to me back then. I always respected him in school because he worked hard and was a great athlete. I would never have thought the Lord would impact him through me. This was the moment that I truly realized that people are watching you even when you do not know they are. That is why it is important to be a person who lives life with intention, integrity, and purpose. Most importantly a purpose in the Lord, because in the Lord there is hope not only in this world, but beyond it.

I Pray

I pray that as you read these God stories, that you were encouraged in the Lord. I pray you know that no matter what age you are that the Lord can use you to impact others.

Matthew 5:16 says, *"In the same way, let your light shine before others, that they may see your good deeds and glorify your father in heaven."*

1 Timothy 4:12 says, *"Don't let anyone look down on you because you are young, but set an example for the believers in speech, in conduct, in love, in faith, and in purity."* I pray that all young people would believe these scriptures and credit God for being able to be a light and set an example to begin with. I pray that all young people around the world and those reading this would be strengthened in the Lord and have the boldness to stand for Christ in all areas of their life, Amen.

LAYING A FOUNDATION OF COMMUNITY

Choosing OSU

The summer going into my senior year of high school I had twenty-five college football offers. I decided to commit to The Ohio State University that summer. We also decided as a family that enrolling early (January 2018) would be the best decision for me. I chose OSU because they had an elite football program with a winning tradition, competition that would make me a better player, and a huge alumni base I could connect with beyond the gridiron. One other thing that stood out to me was that they did not sell me the dream that other programs sold me, but they expressed the truth about how hard I would have to work to see success. This attracted me even more to OSU because I desired to work hard and be pushed to my best.

When someone asked me why I committed to OSU, these were the explanations that I would give them. Although, as my family and I began to search for a community of believers that I could connect with when I got to school, this too became a point of emphasis when I explained the reasons I chose OSU. Little did I know the impact that a community of believers would have on me and my growth in Christ.

Why Lay a Foundation of Community

"The physical presence of other Christians is a source of incomparable joy and strength to the believer."
- Dietrich Bonhoeffer

As believers in Christ, we know that Jesus is the foundation of our faith and salvation, period. 1 Corinthians 3:11 says, *"For no one can lay a foundation other than the one already laid, which is Jesus Christ."* As believers the foundation of our faith and salvation is not rooted in any church building, pastor, denomination, or anything else in this world as those things cannot save you. Our faith and confidence are not even rooted in ourselves on our best day. Isaiah 64:6 says, *"All of us have become like one who is unclean, and all our righteous acts are like filthy rags."* There is no amount of good works we can do to receive eternal life, rather our eternal security is a gift we have been given through the work of Jesus Christ alone. Ephesians 2:8 writes, *"For it is by grace you have been saved, through faith—and this is not from yourselves, it is the gift of God—not by works, so that no one can boast."*

So, in this chapter when I talk about laying a foundation, I am not speaking about laying the foundation of faith in Christ and salvation but the intentional act of connecting with other believers. As believers who already have salvation through Jesus, we are commanded to be in community with other believers to help us grow. Solo Christianity is not the will of God for our lives. Proverbs 27:17 says, *"As iron sharpens iron, so one person sharpens another."* Let me ask, how can we be sharpened by ourselves? Hebrews 10:24-25 says, *"And let us consider how we can spur each other on toward love and good deeds, not giving up meeting together, as some are in the habit of doing, but encouraging one another—and all the more as you see the Day approaching."*

So, with this understanding in mind, I decided to lay a foundation of community before even arriving on campus. This decision turned out to have a greater impact on my relationship with Christ and my college experience than I ever imagined. So, in the rest of this chapter you are going to read about how I laid a foundation of community that I was able to grow and build on. I pray that it will encourage you all to do the same.

Finding A Church Home

One piece to laying a foundation of community was to find a church home before I enrolled at OSU. Of course, it would still be my choice if I went or not, but at least it was treated as a priority right off the bat. It helped set the tone for my college experience. In the search for a church home in Ohio my family and I researched churches in the

Columbus area that had strong values and biblical teaching. It was important to find a place where I could be discipled and continue to grow spiritually. When thinking through what church I would choose we remembered something. We forgot that our pastor here in Murfreesboro Tennessee had a brother named Doyle who pastored at a church in Columbus called The Church Next Door. So, the next time we visited OSU, we attended that church. When we attended, we felt right at home and the service was great and most importantly we were fed with the truth. After service, my family and I introduced ourselves to Pastor Doyle. We shared with him that we were from Murfreesboro Tennessee where his brother is our pastor. He expressed his fondness for Murfreesboro Tennessee as he grew up there and visits there on occasion. So, we instantly had a connection as we were both from the same hometown. I told him that I would be enrolling into OSU the next spring. He was glad to hear that and joyfully welcomed me to attend the church on the weekends when I enrolled.

He then introduced us to an older couple at the church named Bob and Elaine who pretty much became my surrogate grandparents. Bob and Elaine were so generous and were willing to open their home to my family when they came up on weekends for my football games. This allowed my parents not to worry about finding a place to stay along with my two siblings when they came up from Tennessee. Not only did they open their house to my family, but they treated me like family as well. They frequently welcomed me to their home and invited me to their family events and gatherings during my time at OSU. Not to mention all the home cooked meals I got to enjoy. They were always a resource if I ever needed anything and a place I could go to get away from the hustle and bustle of school and ball. It was a great way to reenergize myself.

I not only built a great relationship with them but also Pastor Doyle. He took me under his wing and poured into me like a son and still does to this day. He reminded me of my purpose in Christ and helped me to understand the Word of God better. When I ran into an issue while in school or football or had questions about something, I could rely on him as a more mature believer who had great wisdom. He became a father figure in my life and someone that I was highly encouraged by to stay on the straight and narrow and stand firm in Christ.

Team Chaplains

Another piece to laying a foundation of community was meeting Tom and Jim, the OSU football team chaplains. I expressed my desire to continue walking with the Lord and intention to stay connected with other believers. We exchanged numbers and had conversations over the phone before I enrolled. This allowed me to build a relationship with them and encouraged me to keep my mind on Christ when I arrived on campus. The God stories that came from fellowshipping with these two men of God through my years at OSU were incredible and had a profound impact on my faith. These two men had more of an influence on my life than they could know. The doors that opened for me to expand my faith and trust the Lord to do in me what I felt unqualified to do, helped mold me into a bolder ambassador of Jesus Christ.

Athlete Ministry

The next thing my family and I did before I enrolled at OSU was look for a ministry with people my age that I could connect and fellowship with. Fortunately, Tom and Jim, our team chaplains, were the heads of Athletes in Action or AIA. This group was like the high school FCA ministry I was a part of. AIA was focused on helping athletes grow together, walk together, and encourage one another as they pursue Christ in their sport and life. Although, the group did not have a name when I got to OSU because AIA was going through changes. Nonetheless, we still met but we did not have a name anymore, so we took a poll and made a new name. We renamed the group CrossSports. Cool name, right? Can you guess what it means? If not, I will talk about it later.

I believe some of the relationships I made in this ministry will last a lifetime. Knowing that there were other great athletes that knew pursuing Christ was the most important thing was incredibly encouraging for me. Being able to relate to others in the highs and lows of sports helped me continue to lean on the Lord through tough times and not give up. Reminding each other of our identity in Christ helped us not to worship our sport but leverage our sport to be used by God to display His glory through us.

Campus Ministry

Cru Ohio State was another ministry I found as I searched to be in community with people my age. This was a large student ministry that held services on Sunday nights on campus and men's and women's bible studies throughout the week. This was actually one of the ministries that I found out about soon after I enrolled. This ministry was nice to be a part of because it allowed me to connect with believers my age who did not play sports but participated in other things. I got to investigate their lives and connect with them in a unique way. Growing up, many of my friends played football with me or participated in sports. This was a good change of pace for once. I learned to appreciate the many different ways the Lord blesses us to shine his light.

More Community

My faith community in college was not limited to the ministries that I just wrote about. I engaged and connected with more brothers and sisters in Christ in various places as things transpired. As you continue to read, I will share about some of these interactions and their impact. I only shared the ones that I identified for myself either before I enrolled or very soon after I enrolled to give you an example that you can follow. I want to encourage you to lay a foundation and get in community with other believers!

Get In Community!

"Satan always hates Christian fellowship; it is his policy to keep Christians apart. Anything which can divide saints from one another he delights in. He attaches more importance to godly intercourse than we do. Since union is strength, he does his best to promote separation."
- Charles Spurgeon

Many parents think that when they send their kids off to college that it means to release them to do whatever is they will do, and the world somehow will show them the right way to go. This is a dangerous mindset to have. Education is important, but we have to be just as intentional or more intentional about what community we will do life with. Many people go to school with little to no thought of where they will continue to grow their faith and walk with the Lord. God does not call us to be solo Christians. Although, our enemy Satan likes for us to believe we can go solo. We must understand that doing life alongside other believers is important for us to experience encouragement and strengthening in the Lord and to continue fighting the good fight. You can have all the education in the world, but without the Lord guiding you, what is that education worth? Do not sacrifice Christ and community for curriculum. The Barna Group calculates that a staggering 70% of students that go to college who are professing Christians will leave college with little to no faith. Do you as a student or parent want your child to be in that statistic? If not, here is the answer, Proverbs 24:9 says, *"Surely you need guidance to wage war, and victory is won through many advisers."* This guidance starts with the help of the Holy Spirit that we received when we placed faith in Christ, but it does not end there as the Spirit prompts us to be connected to other believers.

So, what is this proverb talking about when it mentions waging war? Ephesians 6:12 says, *"For our struggle is not against flesh and blood, but against the rulers, against the authorities, against the powers of this dark world and against the spiritual forces of evil in the heavenly realms."* These are the forces we are not only facing right now but will face when we go off to school, move locations, or wherever else. This is why we must be clothed with the armor of God (see Ephesians 6:13-17). 1 Peter 5:8 also says, *"Be alert and of sober mind. Your enemy the devil prowls around like a roaring lion looking for someone to devour."* Let me tell you, the devil is looking to devour you (us), and if you (us) are not alert and sober, he will devour you (us). This is why you should not go to college with no protection or guidance, there is a literal war going on in the spiritual realm that is more real and dangerous than any war in the physical. Parents, why would you send your child off to a war they are not prepared for? It is like going into war with no armor or weapon, thinking that you will not get injured or killed. I am not saying force your child to be in community with other believers, because they can choose whatever they want. I am saying it is important to establish a community of believers before they enroll that they can be a part of when they enroll. This sets the foundation for them to experience growth in the Lord and win over the temptations and evils on campus and in the world. It sets a foundation that your child can build on if they so desire. Although, I do want to encourage believers that are already in college and have not laid a foundation of community for themselves to know that you can start to do that now. The benefits of community far outweigh the risk and apprehensions you may have. In the next chapter I will share with you how my community benefitted and impacted me in great ways. Be encouraged!

THE POWER OF COMMUNITY: BUILDING ON THE FOUNDATION

⁵"I am the vine; you are the branches. If you remain in me and I in you, you will bear much fruit; apart from me you can do nothing."
- John 15:5

"An unintentional life accepts everything and does nothing. An intentional life embraces only the things that will add to the mission of significance."
- John C. Maxwell

Building and Growth Takes Intentional Attention

Before I share how community benefited and impacted me in great ways, I want to share more about what it took for me to trust that I could build and grow within that community.

To build something you must have a foundation and trust that foundation. Weak foundations make for weak buildings and weak results. Strong foundations make for strong buildings and strong results. When your core and spine are weak, the rest of your body suffers. When we do not have a plan of how we will stay connected to Jesus and the body of Christ, rather we are going to school or just in life, our building will weaken. We must understand that nothing in life stays the same, it either improves forward or regresses backward. Something either gets better or worse and nothing else. In Genesis 2:15 it says, *"So the Lord God took man and put him in the Garden of Eden to work it and take care of it."* Does it sound like the Garden was just going to flourish on its own? No, it needed someone to take care of it to flourish or it would get out of hand. This is a fact of life, what we give intentional attention to grows. What we do not give intentional attention to dies. The first assignment that was given to man is this; Genesis 1:28 says, *God blessed them and said to them, "Be fruitful and increase in number; fill the earth and subdue it. Rule over the fish in the sea and the birds in the sky and over every living creature that moves on the ground."* What is this telling us? This tells us that God designed us to increase the gifts that He has given us, and rule, govern, and tend to His beautiful creation for its flourishing onto the glory of the Lord. Since our faith and relationship with the Lord is a gift from God, we must give intentional attention to it if we desire it to grow and increase. Notice how God first blessed man and then gave the assignment to be fruitful, increase, fill, subdue, and rule. So, regarding our faith, if we grow it with intentional attention, the glory is the Lord's because God blessed you to do it. Amen?

Trusting the Foundation of Christ

[19]Consequently, you are no longer foreigners and strangers, but fellow citizens with God's people and also members of his household, [20]built on the foundation of the apostles and prophets, with Christ Jesus himself as the chief cornerstone.
- Ephesians 2:19-20

"Any other foundation will fail, but Christ is a sure and steady rock to build your life on."
- Billy Graham

As mentioned before, laying a foundation of community is important, but that does not mean everyone will give intentional attention to building and growing on it. What I mean by this is that people can decide for themselves if they will pursue the Lord or not while in college. And a part of pursuing the Lord is pursuing to be in community with his children to help us grow stronger and faster than we can on our own. You can have all the things in place like where you would go to church, what ministries you would be a part of and still choose another path. This was a choice I had to make when I stepped foot on campus. Will I pursue the Lord or not? I had to decide if I was going to continue to build my faith on the foundation of Jesus and a foundation of community. I knew that I could easily turn left and try something new and have some "college fun" if you will. After all, leveraging the fact that I was an Ohio State football player could have helped me satisfy many worldly and fleshly pleasures. Although, I knew that it would create short-term pleasure but a long-term problem.

As I noted previously, Barna Group estimates 70% of professing Christians fall away when college is said and done. Much of that 70% may have deliberately chosen the short-term pleasure route, and many may have walked into unbelief unknowingly and unintentionally. Either way, that person decided somewhere along the way that unplugging from the source of Christ and encouragement of community was the route for them. And if someone unplugs too many times, it is hard to find that outlet again. So, I decided I was not going to unplug from Christ or community, and I continued to pursue. Although, in my pursuit I noticed something shifted. Something felt different, but what was it? Then I realized my parents were not here with me to take me to church or a small group. I had to do all this from my own inner desire. My parent's lead was no longer a driving force, rather it became my lead. It no longer could be that I believed in Christ because my parents believed in Christ, and that I grew up with it. If you were to ask a Christian why they are Christian, saying "I grew up with it," is the explanation I think most would give. I realized that any other person from a different religion can as well say, I grew up with it too. I thought to myself, why not be a part of any other faith if saying I grew up with it is what also gave validity to all other religions?

In 1 Peter 3:15 it writes, *"But in your hearts revere Christ as Lord. Always be prepared to give an answer to everyone who asks you to give the reason for the hope that you have. But do this with gentleness and respect."* Does it sound like saying "I grew up with it" suffices as a reason for the hope we have? I do not think so. The best answer would be that I am a Christian because Jesus lived a perfect life, died, was buried, and rose again for my sins so that I could be saved. I soon shifted my answer to match that truth. Instead of saying Christian I like to say Christ Follower because that is more direct about who I serve.

I think the reason we say we grew up with it instead of talking about what Jesus did is because we do not believe it enough or because we know it makes people uncomfortable when they hear the name Jesus. The fact is that there is insurmountable evidence and documentation for Jesus's life, death, burial, and resurrection. We should no longer validate our faith by saying I grew up with it, instead we should say that I am a Christ Follower because it is unequivocally true that He lived, died, was buried, and rose again for my sins so that I could be saved. This not only happened, but He said it would happen and he did it out of love for you and me. I do not know about you, but I am following anyone who can pull that off, and Jesus is the only one that did and ever will because He is God.

When my faith and walk with Christ was no longer attached to my parents' faith or that I grew up with it, but truly became my own, the Holy Spirit opened my eyes further than ever before. He gave me more understanding of who God is in my life. It was then that I knew I was personally motivated to pursue Christ and be in community with His children.

Time to Build

My college experience at The Ohio State University was one that challenged me mentally, physically, and spiritually like never before in my life. Student athlete responsibilities required much more effort and attention than in high school, so I had to learn how to use my time wisely. Even though football was the main reason I went to OSU, I knew that school was important, so I did my best to be as intentional about my schoolwork as I was about football. And I certainly knew the most important thing was pursuing the Lord in everything I did. This meant being aware of the presence of God at the football facility, at school, and anywhere else I went. In the previous chapter, I wrote about how I laid a foundation of community to help keep me grounded in the Lord through all my college endeavors. In the rest of this chapter, you will read about how I built on that foundation as I pursued that community and how it impacted me not just to stay grounded but flourish.

CHURCH COMMUNITY

Church Home

As I shared before, I chose The Church Next Door in Columbus as my church home. When I arrived at OSU, I wasted no time getting plugged in and becoming a regular congregant. Although, I attended mostly in the offseason because we practiced on Sundays during the season. Every time I went, I felt welcomed in, and was refreshed when I left. The services were like my church back home. A couple of differences were that the congregation was smaller and had an older demographic of people overall. At first, I did not like that and thought that I should go to a church with a young majority. Although as time passed, it was good to be around some older wiser people. After all, I was around young people all the time in school and sport. The Bible says in Proverbs 13:20, "Walk with the wise and become wise, for a companion of fools suffers harm." This is not to say that all young people are fools or that all older people are wise, but this verse comes to mind when I think about how this church benefited me. There were still young people that went there such as children, teens, young adults, and young couples, but just not as many as I was used to. I do feel that being around that maturity made me more mature as the scripture expressed. For a while I went to this church on my own but as I settled in, I began to invite teammates to come with me on the weekends. It was not until my sophomore year that I got some of them to attend. I will share a great testimony that came out of that later.

One great part about going to church on Sundays was fellowshipping with people after service by going out to eat. I assume you have heard the term "breaking bread." It means to share a meal but also connect on a deeper more meaningful level. Breaking bread with some of my older brothers and sisters in Christ from church was a great way to be encouraged and also give some encouragement.

Serve and be Great!

When I first came to the church during recruiting, Pastor Doyle introduced me and my family to an older couple at the church named Bob and Elaine. Bob and Elaine were an absolute blessing. They welcomed me into their home regularly like a new addition to their family. They lived on a farm about 40 minutes away from campus, so when I went to their house it felt like a getaway. Although, with my schedule I could not go a ton, but when I did, it was always good cooking. Elaine could cook such amazing meals. The thing that rubbed off on me the most about them was their generosity and servant lifestyle. They would always be doing something for someone else. That is why they were so joyful because they constantly served others.

We all know that serving others creates that since of self-worth. I believe this feeling stems from the fact that it is the will of God for our lives to serve others. In Matthew chapter 20 Jesus addresses his disciples to do as he does by taking a posture of humbleness and position of servant hood.

Matthew 20:25-28 writes, "Jesus called them together and said, *"You know that the rulers of the Gentiles Lord it over them, and their high officials exercise authority over them. Not so with you. Instead, whoever wants to become great among you must be your servant, and whoever wants to be first must be your slave— just as the Son of Man did not come to be served, but to serve, and to give his life as a ransom for many."*

Bob and Elaine lived out this verse well, so they were a fitting example for me to see what commitment to serving others looked like. They challenged me to think of ways I could serve others more. Jesus did say that if you want to become great, then serve. Bob and Elaine were certainly great in the community and highly respected because of how they gave of their time, talent, and efforts. As you continue to read, I will share more about how Bob and Elaine inspired me to serve and live out Matthew 20 more fully.

Guidance

In the last chapter, I mentioned that pastor Doyle's brother was my hometown pastor. I thought to myself, what are the odds that I would be at this church where the pastor is the brother of the pastor I grew up listening to. How many brothers do you know that are both pastors? As I listened to his sermons, I thought he was a great teacher with a real sense of humor. I frequently had talks with him after services discussing the message or just having good friendly conversation. We began to develop a relationship. Through conversation we connected and spent time together outside of the four walls of the church. When I had the time to have dinner with him and his wife Jennifer or just talk, I always left feeling encouraged to walk tall in Christ and supported in my endeavors. Pastor Doyle and Jennifer became mentors of mine as they freely gave their time to pour into me. They always left their door open to help me with anything I needed and were also willing to be a helping hand to any other teammates. I know you may be thinking that they did this just to get close to OSU football players. Although I personally do not believe that. They desired to spread light to wherever they went and whoever they encountered. The way they poured into me helped me to better pour into my teammates and others. Even though I am a couple years removed from college, they continue to pour into me. They encouraged me to write this book. So, after prayer and inquiring, here I am. I believe I will always have a relationship with them moving forward. Their guidance helped me wage war on the enemy that was trying to take me out, the world that was trying to bring me down, and the temptations that tried to distract me.

Here is a verse about waging war that we discussed in the last chapter. Proverbs 24:6 says, *"Surely you need guidance to wage war, and victory is won through many advisors."* Have you heard of the phrase "if you want something done right, do it yourself?" This is what the world wants us to believe, it is a lie from the enemy. This is one of the pieces of bait Satan used to deceive Eve in the Garden of Eden (see Genesis 3:4-6). It is considered the pride of life. 1 John 2:16 says, *"For everything in the world—the lust of the flesh, the lust of the eye, and the pride of life—comes from the world."* The saying "if you want something done right, do it yourself" I believe is mostly rooted in the pride of life. We see that God's Word emphasizes guidance and connection with believers as a pivotal piece to our success and flourishing as his creations and children. So, we should say this instead; "If you want to win, get wisdom and guidance." I won in my faith during college through the wisdom and guidance of the Holy Spirit. I also won because of the guidance and wisdom from believers in Christ equipped to help me through the arena of life God placed me. In this case I am talking about Pastor Doyle, his wife Jennifer, Bob, Elaine, and others I will mention in this book.

Since I connected to these people, I was more connected to God. And as I was more connected to God, I was more disconnected from the temptations of "the college life" of partying, drinking, sleeping around, staying out late, and embracing the pleasures of my flesh and this world. This is exactly what happens to people who do not have "many advisors" as the Proverb mentioned. Without guidance and advisors, the motivation to stay on the straight and narrow is much harder.

It is like starting a business without knowledge of the business. And when you start the business, you run it by yourself. When you run the business by yourself the probability of burning out or just straight up failing is much greater than if you had mentors and others to work the business with you. Success comes with mentors and partners. They help us avoid pitfalls that could come our way. And if you do find yourself falling, you can quickly recover as the people around you can help restore you. So, if you go at it alone in this walk of faith, you may fall into a pit that will be hard to get out of by yourself. With the help of the Holy Spirit and community with believers in Christ, I was able to wage war against the physical and spiritual darkness of this world and win. I am still winning. Let me leave you with two verses from King Solomon, the wisest man to ever live besides Jesus, in Ecclesiastes 4:9-10 he writes, *"Two are better than one, because they have a good return for their labor: If either of them falls down, one can help the other up. But pity anyone who falls and has no one to help them up."* Get in community!

SPORT COMMUNITY

Truth at the Table

My schedule during football season in college was hefty. We easily spent 7 to 8 hours or more in the facility as we worked out in the morning and had meetings and practice later in the day. It was like this Tuesday through Friday. In between workouts and meetings, we went to class. The slot of time for attending class was about 4 hours. I usually left the facility somewhere between 6:30 and 7:30pm. When I got home, I typically had more schoolwork to complete and had to study film and or the playbook to be prepared for my game on the weekend. With this kind of schedule, it was hard for me to find time to connect with a community of believers. This is where Tom and Jim were such a blessing to me and others.

Before, I talked about being aware of the presence of God through everything I did. It was difficult for me at times to be aware of His presence when I had much on my plate that I needed to complete. Sometimes I would get to the end of my days and realize that I had not acknowledge God at all. I know we all have experienced that. Fortunately, Tom and Jim made sure to be there for the players' spiritual edification as they fit in seamlessly with our schedules. During the season, most guys would eat all three meals at the football facility cafeteria. It was free food and all you could eat.

So, Tom and Jim went around to different tables during meals and had 5-to-10-minute bible studies with us. When I tell you they were consistent with these bible studies day in and day out, they were consistent. I cannot remember one day when they did not have a smile on their faces. You could tell they were genuine and cared about all the players. Even though they talked about scripture with us, they did it in such a graceful and humble way that most players were willing to listen. Tom and Jim were such a blessing as they helped me stay grounded in the truth of God's Word amid the busyness of school and football. They helped me keep my mind more on the things above rather than things below and be more aware of God in my daily routine.

God Is Faithful

The consistent bible studies were a reminder of how God is always faithful in showing up, being near, and available for us to always cling to. Psalms 145:17-18 says, *"The Lord is righteous in all his ways and faithful in all he does. The Lord is near to all who call on him, to all who call on him in truth."* Note that the Lord is righteous in all His ways. Righteousness has to do with what is morally right and just. Note that He is faithful in all he does. Faithfulness has to do with loyalty and always showing up for the good of another no matter the condition. Righteousness and faithfulness are in God's character and nature. This means that the best advocate we have is the Lord. This is why the next verse says, "the Lord is near to all who call on him, to all who call on him in truth."

The days that I became overwhelmed and anxious about football, school, or anything else were the days I did not call on God in the truth of His Word. Rather, I called on myself to be and do what only God can be in do. On the other hand, when I did call on him in the truth of His Word, I felt secure in His righteousness, comforted by His faithfulness, and His peace was with me. Philippians 4:6-7 was also an important scripture for me to believe. It says, *"Do not be anxious about anything, but in every situation, by prayer and petition, with thanksgiving, present your requests to God. And the peace of God, which transcends all understanding, will guard your hearts and minds in Christ Jesus."*

During my first year of college football, I struggled with being anxious about messing up a play or embarrassing myself. I would ask myself, "am I good enough?" Philippians 4:6-7 became a key verse for me to trust and believe. When I made a habit of praying before practice, I not only asked God to give me peace, but I expressed thanksgiving in the place God put me. Through this, I not only received the peace of God, but the perspective of God. I began to understand that if he is for me, who or what can be against me? I had to trust that God would give me peace and that I was at OSU for a reason. That reason was because He gave me the ability, talent, and work ethic to be there. In fact, I would not have been there if I were not good enough. And beyond that I am here to give glory to God and represent

Christ in what I do. I realized that the best posture was a posture of weakness, only then was I able to lean on God's strength.

In 2 Corinthians 12:9 the apostle Paul Has a thorn in his flesh tormenting him and Jesus responds by saying, *"My grace is sufficient for you, for my power is made perfect in weakness."*

This thorn that Paul had was there to make him dependent on God's strength and not his own. In other words, his pain had a purpose. Paul then continues to write, *"Therefore I boast all the more gladly in my weaknesses so that Christ's power may rest on me."* Accepting the fact that I was weak is what gave me the power in Christ to be strong.

CrossSports

Another piece of community that gave me great encouragement through football and school was the CrossSports ministry. This was a ministry focused on helping athletes grow together, walk together, and encourage one another as they pursue Christ in sport and life. I mentioned before how we thought of the name CrossSports as we no longer used the name Athletes in Action (AIA). Although, I did not explain what the name meant. The word 'Cross' in the name represents the cross of Christ because He is the center of our faith and holds it all together. The word 'Sports' is there because we play sports. CrossSports represents how we as athletes put Jesus first in everything and allow Him to lead us in our sport. CrossSports also represents men and women across all sports uniting with the motivation to know more of Christ and to make him more known through the gifts he has given us.

Athlete to Athlete

During the football season, the CrossSports group met Wednesdays after practice at 7pm in the athletic facility that connected to our football facility. Tom and his wife Julie were the main ones to head this up, although the group had student representatives and leaders that often emceed and introduced speakers. We got to hear biblical messages, player, and coach testimonies, engage in meaningful thought-provoking discussions, and pray for and encourage one another in the Lord.

There were times in my college career when I felt like I was the only one struggling with something whether physical or mental. In my four years playing college football I underwent two surgeries, had a concussion, twisted ankles, and strained and pulled muscles. I felt like it was one thing after the next and it broke me down. In sport culture we learn to bottle all that away because it is a sign of weakness, and you cannot be weak and win. So, we do not share our pains and therefore we think we are alone not knowing that the person next to us could just as well be thinking and experiencing something similar. At CrossSports, these were the topics that we got to discuss and share about. When one person would open up, another would open up, and another. The next thing you know, we are breaking the ice and connecting more deeply. We became encouraged because we saw that we were not alone in the struggles of our journeys. Not only did we see that we were not alone but that we were all still here making it through by the grace of God. With that in mind, let me tell you an incredible story of how CJ, a teammate and CrossSports leader planted a seed of faith in me during a rough moment.

A Seed of Faith

March of my junior year I was optimistic going into spring practice. I just came off a solid sophomore year as a backup running back earning 3rd team all big ten honors. On our first day of practice something happened that I never expected. As I went for a route and caught the ball, I turned up field and something popped in the back of my leg, and I fell. I initially looked back because I thought someone kicked me. I tried to get up and walk but there was no strength in my leg, so I fell back to the ground. They helped me into the training room where they examined me. I believe the training staff knew what happened but were hesitant to say what it was because it was a severe injury. I had to wait for an MRI to get the final assessment. After an MRI scan, the doctor told me I suffered a torn Achilles tendon. At this point I was frustrated and did not understand why or how this happened. The doctors told me it would take seven to nine months to heal, so I would probably miss some of the 2020 season.

A day or two later I was lying in our team athletic training room and my dad sat beside me. CJ, a teammate of mine and a CrossSports leader at the time, encouraged me and said, "You are going to have the fastest comeback story we have ever seen." CJ had faith that I would heal faster than what science and the doctor said. I shook his hand in agreement with that statement of faith. CJ planted a seed of faith in me that moved me to dominate my recovery plan. My commitment to the treatment program my athletic trainers gave me only granted me a chance to recover faster than the doctor said. I would have to see how my body responded. With everything locked down because of Covid, I did most of my recovery on my own in my apartment. I had to be creative and use what I had to get the work done. For example, I took a towel and placed food cans and other heavy items on it to do toe crunches. I even used my toilet to do step ups. The most important thing I had during this process was faith that the Lord can do what they said cannot be done. Guess what happened, six months later I made a full recovery just in time for the 2020 season. Mind you that season was delayed, and our first game was not until October, but I was ready.

There is a great lesson in this story that is important for us to understand. Yes, I had faith that I would recover quickly but this faith was not alone, but it was followed by action. James 2:17 says, *"In the same way, faith by itself, if not accompanied by action, is dead."* When we have faith that a certain outcome will happen, our actions should tell us, "I expect it to happen." If our actions do not say that to us when we profess faith in a particular outcome, then we probably do not have faith. Faith is the seed of action.

This experience has graced me to help several others that have gone through the same injury to be encouraged that they can overcome it and come back strong. In fact this applies to all the injuries I have had. Anytime we overcome a trial, we can show the next person how they can too. These trials could be anything you have faced or are facing, not just injuries.

To bring this home more, let us look at a scripture that emphasizes the victory we have in Christ no matter the circumstance. At the end of Romans 8, Paul writes to the church in Rome encouraging them through the trials and hardships they face for the sake of Christ. He reminds them of the victory that they have already received even when their circumstances say the opposite. In Romans 8:37-39 Paul writes, *"No, in all these things we are more than conquerors through him who loved us. For I am convinced that neither death nor life, neither angels nor demons, neither the present nor the future, nor any power, neither height nor depth, nor anything else in all creation, will be able to separate us from the love of God that is in Christ Jesus our*

Lord." How beautiful is that truth. Notice that we are not just conquerors, but we are more than conquerors, we are beyond victorious. We are more than conquerors over any and all physical (anything you can see) circumstances and spiritual (anything you cannot see) attacks that we will experience in our life.

Confident in Identity

Considering sports, careers, or our pursuits, understanding our identity in Christ is a pivotal perspective for us to stand firm and unwavered in the Lord. In the CrossSports ministry, this was a common topic of discussion. It was extremely easy as a high-level athlete to place my identity, value, and worth in what I did rather than what Jesus did. Understanding that what I did was of no account to my worth, but it is what Jesus did that made me worthy was pivotal. That understanding positioned me to play free from the worry of being perfect in football because what truly matters is that I am perfect in Christ. I am not saying we should not strive to be our perfect selves in our pursuits, because we do honor the Lord through our efforts. Although, this should not be the driving force that dictates our joy and peace in this world.

CrossSports was an outlet for me to stay grounded in that truth. I do have to say that I am not perfect at this and still must work on it today. Although, I am grateful to the

Holy Spirit and the community of people I still have around me to encourage and remind me of my identity in Christ.

CAMPUS COMMUNITY

The Body of Christ

Cru Ohio State was another ministry that I was involved with during my time in college. Cru services were on Sunday evenings at a concert venue on campus. I was off Sunday evenings in football season, so this worked great with my schedule. I did not know anyone when I first attended Cru. I went, worshipped, listen to the sermon, and left. After a few times attending Cru, I finally opened my mouth and conversed with people. I connected with some of my fellow buckeyes and plugged into one of the men's evening bible studies held in the week. Here we were able to go deep into the Word of God together and talk about the things that we struggled with and what the Lord had been personally showing us. The topics we discussed here were more centered around being a student at OSU and how to navigate the paths of our studies and educational pursuits.

Being a part of the Cru campus ministry showed me that the body of Christ consists of all types of people with different gifts to serve different people. It showed me that just because I am a high caliber athlete that a hundred thousand people watch in the stadium, does not mean that what I do is more significant than what someone else is doing. Sometimes as athletes we shy away from community with people pursuing different things than we are. I agree that there is wisdom in that at times. Although when we connect with believers with different passions, we can really learn to appreciate all the gifts God has given each of us to use for his glory. At least that is what I discovered.

In Romans 12:3-5 the apostle Paul writes, *"For by the grace given me I say to every one of you: Do not think of yourself more highly than you ought, but rather think of yourself with sober judgment, in accordance with the faith God has distributed to each of you. For just as each of us has one body with many members, and these members do not all have the same function, so in Christ we, though many, form one body, and each member belongs to all the others."* We all know that our physical bodies have distinct parts with distinct functions and purposes. When one part of the body hurts or is not functioning correctly, the other parts work to bring healing to the part in need. The reason that the body works this way is because it recognizes the other parts' value. It knows that there is an important function that it needs to do. So, when the other parts help heal the hurt part to function the way it is purposed to, it allows the whole body to operate optimally. This is what it means to be a part of the body of Christ (our community). Do we love and value our fellow believers enough to stand by, encourage, and bring healing to them so they can better function in their purpose?

Alex, my Cru small group leader lived out that Romans 12 verse well. He was someone who always made sure others were encouraged by listening and then edifying them in the place they were in. All year around he regularly reached out to me to genuinely see how I was. Sometimes we overlook the trivial things like shooting someone a text and asking how they are. They may not be vulnerable at first, but once you have sent a few messages overtime asking how they are, they see that you really care and usually feel more comfortable opening up. Something that helps me to encourage others more is to reach out to a person as soon as I think of them. You know how we think of a person and wonder how they are but never reach out to them? What if every time we thought of someone, we decided to reach out and see how they were doing? I am not talking about in an annoying way like blowing up their phone. The occasional text, talk on the phone, or meet up should suffice. The beauty of being in God's family is that you have brothers and sisters everywhere that you can fight with and stand beside because we are all facing the same enemy and opposition.

In 1 Peter 5:9 it says, *"Resist him, standing firm in the faith, because you know that the family of believers throughout the world is undergoing the same kind of sufferings."* The enemy wants us to believe we are alone and convince us that isolation equals safety. Think of Jesus, instead of isolating, hiding, and covering himself, he became vulnerable, naked, and uncovered. This act of nakedness and exposure resulted in our salvation and freedom in him. The word isolation means to lock oneself away and separate from the world. God did not make Eve for Adam so that they could isolate themselves from each other. God did not command them to be fruitful and multiply so they could hide away from each other. To let his kingdom come and his will be done on earth as it is in heaven, we must do it together. Amen? So, get in community!

Platformed to Point to God

Cru Ohio State was similar to CrossSports as they gave students the opportunity to share their testimonies of how they came to faith in Jesus. I was blessed to do this twice my sophomore year. Though the second time was better than the first because I did it alongside a handful of my teammates. CJ, my teammate and CrossSports leader was also there. We all sat on stage and answered questions about how the Lord has blessed us to do what we do. It was a great opportunity to use our platform and encourage fellow buckeyes that even the "celebrities" of the city can be humble and acknowledge that it is the man above that empowers us. No matter if you are a high caliber athlete, businessperson, entrepreneur, mechanic, engineer, architect, doctor, nurse, or anything else, you are to use that gift to point others to Christ and not yourself. Sorry not sorry to say this, but we are not that special, but God is.

COMMUNITY CONTINUED

"There is brotherhood within the body of believers, and the Lord Jesus is the common denominator. Friendship and fellowship are the legal tender among believers. "
- J. Vernon McGee

An Unexpected Invite

The summer of my first year of college, I was invited to Rock City Church in Columbus as there were a handful of teammates that attended. We had a coach who invited players over to his house for breakfast before service. I was told that Pastor Chad, the church pastor, was well con- nected with our football team through a relationship with our head coach Urban Meyer. I think that was the reason some of the guys went there. At that time, I did not really know Pastor Chad as I have not heard him speak much or met him. Although, when the football season came around, he occasionally spoke to our team. He shared messages of faith and motivation with us on Friday nights before a game. It was in our weekly schedule on Friday nights to eat dinner together as a team and then hear a message of faith and motivation. Not everyone listened as this was not mandatory, but it was refreshing that my teammates and I could listen to these kinds of messages before games every weekend. It was one of my favorite things we did to prepare.

(Really quick, before I keep going, I must mention something. When we had home games, we ate dinner together as a team at the Scarlet Golf Course at The Ohio State University. Let me tell you, you will not find a place with better cinnamon rolls than the ones they had here. You can ask any Ohio State football player about these rolls, and I guarantee a smile. You are reading this sometime after I wrote it, but you can bet that when I was writing this my mouth watered.)

Anyway, I digress. As I heard more of Pastor Chad speak, Rock City Church became my second church home. Like Pastor Doyle at The Church Next Door, Pastor Chad was very hospitable. One weekend my dad and sister came to visit, and we all went to Rock City. After the service Pastor Chad invited us into his office and we fellowshipped with him and his wife. We did not know he would invite us into his office before we went in, so it was a pleasant surprise. I had already spent some time with pastor at this point, but my dad had never met him. Pastor took the time to meet my dad and sister when he did not have to. He engaged with us and had a genuine interest in getting to know my family. I truly felt blessed by God to be in community with his children. As I looked at the community of believers, I connected with in all aspects of my college life, I felt blessed to be able to fellowship with so many brothers and sisters in Christ. I thought to myself, "how could I ever be in need with this much love and support?" I felt wealthy spiritually in the Lord and his people.

Although, the Lord also blessed me with brothers in Christ that I could walk with in a more intimate way. I am talking about brothers I could do life with on a deeper level and not just surface. That was in fact a prayer of mine throughout my freshman year as I did not have that kind of relationship but desired it. So, in the next chapter I want to share a collection of stories of how I gained these intimate friendships (brothers in Christ) and how we were salt and light in the world around us.

Choose Your Friends Wisely

As believers we ought to be careful about who we are friends with and who we do life with. As true followers of Christ we do not just want a professing Christian as a friend but a devoted Christ follower that we can have deep fellowship with. We should desire to have brothers or sisters in Christ who are eager to know him and live out his way and not the way of the world. No, we should not think of a perfect person but someone that is obviously different from the world and who strive to do God's will. What I am saying is we need to have friends with which we are equally yoked. I believe that the closer we want someone to be in our lives, the more equally yoked they should be.

In 2 Corinthians 6:14 it says, *"Do not be yoked together with unbelievers. For what do righteousness and wickedness have in common? Or what fellowship can light have with darkness?"* This is a verse that I think hits home for many of us. I say this because it can be hard to sever ties with old friends or even family that only tempt us to do wrong and take us further from God rather than closer. As believers in Christ, we are called to be light, and light cannot bond with darkness. One will always try and cancel the other out. Instead, when light bonds with light, it is free to shine even brighter, and the brighter they shine together, darkness begins to leave. The phrase "choose your friends wisely" is also a great correlation here, and we all know what that means. Proverbs 12:26 says, *"The righteous choose their friends carefully, but the way of the wicked leads them astray."* This is again, why it is important to be in community with other believers in Christ. So, get in community!

SHINE GOD'S LIGHT & MAKE KINGDOM IMPACT!

¹³ "You are the salt of the earth. But if the salt loses its saltiness, how can it be made salty again? It is no longer good for anything, except to be thrown out and trampled underfoot. ¹⁴ "You are the light of the world. A town built on a hill cannot be hidden. ¹⁵ Neither do people light a lamp and put it under a bowl. Instead they put it on its stand, and it gives light to everyone in the house. ¹⁶ In the same way, let your light shine before others, that they may see your good deeds and glorify your Father in heaven.
- Matthew 5:13-16

We should not ask, 'What is wrong with the world?' for that diagnosis has already been given. Rather we should ask, "What has happened to salt and light?
- John Stott

We Are Salt

In Matthew 5:13 Jesus says, *"You are the salt of the earth. But if the salt loses its saltiness, how can it be made salty*

So, what does Jesus mean when he says we are the salt of the earth? Well, we know salt preserves things and as believers we are to preserve the earth from the rot of evil by doing good. Proverbs 28:5 says, *"Evildoers do not understand what is right, but those who seek the Lord understand it fully."* Imagine a world where no one sought the Lord, it would be hell. We as believers are to show the world what is right and good and pleasing to the Lord our creator for the preservation of the earth.

In Exodus and Leviticus salt was used to purify offerings to the Lord. In 2 Kings 2, Elisha used salt to heal and purify bad water. An everlasting covenant of salt was made between the Lord and Aaron in Numbers 18 and with David in 2 Chronicles 13. So, in the Bible, salt was used to purify and cleanse, heal, and restore, and make covenants to preserve an agreement. As believers we must ask ourselves, "am I living a pure life according to what God says?" "Am I bringing healing and restoration to the places and people I encounter? "Am I spreading the good news of the new covenant, which is the gospel of Jesus Christ?" If we are not, then we should. It should be done from a place of great love for the Father and love for others as ourselves. Jesus says if salt loses it saltiness, it is good for nothing except to be thrown out and trampled underfoot. In Christ, we are made to be salty and bring a holy flavor to the places we go. Why do we claim to follow Jesus if we are not being who he says we are to be?

We Are Light

In Matthew 5:14-16 Jesus says, *"You are the light of the world. A town built on a hill cannot be hidden. Neither do people light a lamp and put it under a bowl. Instead, they put it on its stand, and it gives light to everyone in the house. In the same way, let your light shine before others, that they may see your good deeds and glorify your Father in heaven."*

So, according to what Jesus says and what we already know about light, it cannot be hidden, and it gives light to everyone. As believers our light cannot be hidden unless we dim it and put a bowl over it. If we allow this light God placed in us to shine, it can move people to glorify him. Although, it can also do the opposite. We all remember that time growing up when we were sleeping, and someone busted in and turned on the lights. Wasn't that frustrating? Did you cover yourself even more under the blankets? I am guessing you did. This is how some people will react to the light we possess. They will hate it and go further into hiding because it exposes that they are sleeping and need to wake up. On the other hand, those who are awake or are waking up love the light and will run towards it because they know they cannot sleep forever, there would be no purpose or progression in that. They know that the light is the source of life keeping them safe and showing the way. That light is God and his truth.

There are several instances in the Bible where the usage of light can help us understand what it means to be light. Let us look at two of them. In Genesis 1:16 it says, *"God made two great lights—the greater light to govern the day and the lesser light to govern the night."* On the fourth day of creation, God set lights in the sky that we know as the sun and the moon. He assigned the sun to govern or rule the day and assigned the moon to govern or rule the night. It is interesting that at night it is dark, but God put a light in it to rule it. In God's creation, light always wins, and darkness cannot overcome it. Also, you may already know that the moon does not emit its own light but merely reflects the light of the sun. The moon is a great representation of how we as believers are made to be lights. As the sun uses the moon to reflect its light in the darkness of the night, so God uses his children to reflect his light in the darkness of the world.

Let us look at the second example. When Jesus was born, there was a star that led three wise men (magi) to Jesus. In Matthew 2:9-11 it writes, *"they went on their way, and the star they had seen when it rose went ahead of them until it stopped over the place where the child was. When they saw the star, they were overjoyed. On coming to the house, they saw the child with his mother Mary, and they bowed down and worshiped him."* Do you notice how a light (the star) rose and led them to Jesus? I believe this is a parallel to Matthew 5:14-16. We as believers are to be like the moon and reflect Gods light in a dark world. We are to be like the lamp on its stand giving light to everyone, like a star rising up showing the way to Jesus. Amen?

Kingdom Impact

To have kingdom impact, we must be salt and light. When we are salty and let our light shine, we are pointing people to the truth of Jesus Christ and his love that can preserve another person's life from decay (death).

Jesus says to *"let your light shine before others, that they may see your good deeds and glorify your Father in heaven."*

This very statement implies that some of us will not use the light we have been given. If we have been given such a great light, we should be eager to spread it and light it up. And if we are connected to other believers (community) who also have that light, it will help us shine brighter.

Mission Across the World

My sophomore year, there was an opportunity for a few football players to do something incredibly special. Tom and Jim were hosting a mission trip to East Asia through the

CrossSports Ministry. Although, only a few players could go. I thought this was a great opportunity, and I wanted to join them. I always thought that going on a mission trip would be an amazing experience. There were three players and a strength coach intern that went on the mission trip. Thankfully, I was one of those guys. Derrick was one of the other players I went with who I would soon build a great relationship with as a brother in Christ. If you have never been on a plane overseas before, these flights are long, and the planes are big. It took us well over twenty hours to arrive at our destination. When we arrived, I remember everyone gazing at and taking pictures of Derrick like he was a monument. He is 6'4" and I guess the people there have never seen anyone that tall before. I am sure we were all quite tall in their eyes. Throughout the trip we had an interpreter as there was a language barrier. While we were there, we taught the kids how to play football and had a flag football tournament. I believe my team won; I think. It was amazing how fast they learned and how coachable they were despite a language barrier. We also shared in their culture through food and art. Most importantly we shared the truth and love of Christ and our testimonies. Again, it amazed me how receptive they were to all we taught them and did with them.

There were two particular kids there that I took a liking to and vice versa. Even though we did not speak the same language, we became friends. Those kids were always around me; it was like having an additional set of younger siblings. To bring joy and a smile to kids' faces over 8,000 miles from home was an amazing blessing for our lives. To shine the light of the Lord on those kids through deed and word is something I would never have imagined I would be graced to do. I would not have been able to do it if I were not connected with Tom and Jim (a piece of my community).

The Lord blessed us dearly to take the good news to a place that desperately needed more of it. He reminded us of how blessed we are in the states to each stand in our own values and express them boldly without fear of dire consequences. When it was time for us to head back home, it was difficult to say goodbye to all the kids we spent time with. We knew that it was likely the last time we would ever see them. As we made our way back, all of us rehashed our experience talking about the sites we saw, the kids we interacted with, all the food we tried (including McDonalds), and the faith we grew. It was a rememberable experience for all of us and an opportunity to be a light in the world across the world.

Mission Columbus

This mission trip to East Asia would not be the only outreach that I would do. Tom and Jim connected me and my teammate Derrick to a man named Tim Brown. Tim Brown was the FCA camp director of Columbus City Schools. He opened the door for us to go into the heart of Columbus and share our faith and football journeys with inner-city school students. These students picked our brains and asked us questions about our successes to help their journeys. We talked about the discipline it took to earn an opportunity to play at the highest level of college football. We also emphasized the importance of their studies and education and how that played a role in us having the opportunity to be at OSU. Most importantly, we encouraged them in the light of the Lord and expressed that the most success and wealth they could ever have, is found in entrusting themselves to the Lord Jesus Christ. We emphasized the peace that can be had through Jesus Christ no matter the circumstances and obstacles of life. We shared that in Christ, we always win.

Through outreach, Derrick and I shined the Lord's light brighter together. We understood more fully that when we practiced serving, blessing, and loving the people around us, we in turn are blessed. We all were indeed blessed to serve and share the love of God with the kids both in East Asia and inner-city Columbus. Only the Lord knew what it may have done for the life of one of his image bearers, we were just grateful to plant a seed of truth.

An Answered Prayer

As I mentioned previously, I prayed to the Lord for a brother in Christ that I could fellowship with on a deeper level. This is not to say there were no Christ followers on the team, I just had not connected with them on that level yet. Spring of my sophomore year, I connected with my teammate Derrick on the mission trip to East Asia and we enjoyed each other's company. So, when we got back home, we continued to foster our relationship. He invited me to a bible study led by his dad where we all fellowshipped with one another. His dad was an animated character that had great zeal for the Lord. Derrick and I even did more outreach together serving those in the community. I saw that he was a devoted believer in Christ and well-studied. We also had what I like to remember as post-practice therapy sessions. Do let me explain.

Have you ever beat yourself up about a bad grade or performance you had at work, school, or something else? Well, I used to beat myself up when I had a bad practice or performed below the standard, and our team standard was not average but elite. I had to quickly learn that when you are competing at the highest level of something, there is no time to sulk in what happened before, but only focus on what can be done presently to rise above it. If I do not, then one bad practice will turn into two and two into three and so forth. My teammate Derrick helped me to see that. He helped me gain a positive perspective on a seemingly only negative situation. There are always two sides to any story, it just depends on what side we choose to focus on. Derrick always showed me that positive side of the situation. I not only was encouraged and strengthened by his friendship, but I got to encourage and strengthen him as well. It was one brother sharpening another. Derrick became a strong friend and brother in Christ that I had many great faith filled experiences with. My community just got a little bigger. The Lord answered my prayer, and I now had a brother on Christ I fellowshipped with on a deeper level.

When thinking back on this, I saw that the Lord did not answer my prayer without any effort on my part. I had to be in community and literally go on a mission trip to initiate a relationship with Derrick. I am not saying you will have to go on a mission trip to find a brother or sister in Christ and a potential lifelong friend, but I know you will not find one spending time together with people who do not follow Christ. So, get in community with believers!

The Invitation

God continued to answer my prayer, but again not without action on my part. Every year, new players enroll and arrive on campus bright eyed and bushy tailed. My sophomore year, there was one particular player that arrived at OSU that I would not have thought I would connect with. I remember first talking with him in our facility cafeteria. His name was Cormontae and was from West Tennessee. This was a point of commonality as I told him I was from Tennessee as well. Although we never knew of each other before this point, we knew about one another's high school and some of the same players from the state. We conversed about our football teams and the championships we won or lack thereof. At that time there were three players from Tennessee on the OSU football team, and it was nice to have another fellow Tennessean on board. Even though Cormontae and I grew up in the same state and shared some commonalities, I did not think our personalities meshed very well. Although, I was mistaken. Cormontae and I began to have regular conversations in the team cafeteria. We talked about everything from ball, school, family, and upbringing. I also shared Christ with him and invited him to attend the Church Next Door with me. Fortunately, he was open to coming because he desired to know God more but did not know where to start. So, we attended church together on Sundays during the offseason. He instantly received love from Pastor Doyle, Jennifer, and Bob and Elaine. In our spare time we would go to each other's apartment to hang out and chat as we grew a friendship.

In my apartment I had sticky notes with scriptures on them that I put on the doors and bed headboard. I did this so that when I woke up or just hanging out in my apartment I would always be reminded of God's truth. This was a great way to share with him how God's word grounds us and gives us a God perspective and not a world perspective. Instead of waking up to screens, social media, and entertainment, I made it hard for myself not to wake up to the truth, which is God's word. Like the story with Kyle in high school, I shared scripture with him and talked about the nature of God. I was blessed that the Lord put him in my life to disciple and show him the awesomeness of Jesus.

Several months later Cormontae and I were in my car having a conversation about what it means to be a child of God trusting in Christ alone as Lord and Savior. It was at that time that he accepted the Lord into his life and received the Holy Spirit. I was so excited for him that he accepted the call to entrust his life to the Lord. It was the best decision he could make. Now, he has the privilege of partaking in the unmeasurable gift of fellowship and eternal life with the Creator, and also gained an eternal family of brothers and sisters in Christ. Like Kyle, I could see a change in him over time, I knew the Holy Spirit was working on him because his words, actions, and desires were pointing more towards righteousness and obedience to God.

Imagine if I had just gone with my original thought of our personalities not meshing well, I may not have seen the Lord move the way he did in Cormontae's life. Mind you, I was just living my life to honor the Lord and I did not force anything on Cormontae or stuff the Bible down his throat. It was the Lord doing all the heavy lifting behind the scenes.

As Cormontae continued to come with me to church, my community became his community. Pastor Doyle, Jennifer, Bob, Elaine, and others loved on him and prayed for him. He eventually was baptized at the Church Next Door. He became a brother in Christ that I had deep fellowship with. My community just got a little bigger. Sometime later, I went to Cormontae's apartment and saw something familiar, there were scriptures on the wall. It was heartwarming to see that. He said he was inspired when he saw the scriptures on the wall in my apartment. I was amazed at how God used our encounters, because like I said before, I just lived life to honor the Lord through the help of the Holy Spirit.

As believers, our very day to day lives should point to the light of Christ and not just on Sundays or special events. When you live a life close to Christ, you have no choice but to shine when people are near you. I am joyful that Cormontae now has that same light that he can shine, which is the light of Christ.

Radical Shift

Around the time I first met Cormontae, Kam another one of my teammates had a radical conversion to faith in Christ. I cannot tell his story but all I can say is that it is amazing. He was as far as you thought someone could be from the Lord, but that did not keep God from touching his life and showing him the truth of Jesus. God can take someone from the grave and bring them to glory, and that is what he did with Kam. Kam not only entrusted his life to Christ, but he brought a friend with him. That friend he brought was also a teammate of ours named Xavier. The Holy Spirit showed both of them the mystery of Christ and their witness had a great impact on the OSU football team. They invited several of us players to see them get baptized at their church. Many teammates showed up, and not just the ones who professed faith but also some that were apprehensive. I knew I could not miss this great moment. Before they were baptized, they got on stage and spoke about how the Lord changed their life. I have never heard such anointed words from people who just began believing in Christ. It was like they were already well studied in the holy scriptures. The Holy Spirit quickened their mind and gave them speech that many "seasoned believers" do not have. This reminds me of Proverbs 9:10 which says, *"The fear of the Lord is the beginning of wisdom, and knowledge of the Holy One is understanding."* Also, in 1 Corinthians 2:11-13 it says, *"no one knows the thoughts of God except the Spirit of God. What we have received is not the spirit of the world, but the Spirit who is from God, so that we may understand what God has freely given us. This is what we speak, not in words taught us by human wisdom but in words taught by the Spirit, explaining spiritual realities with Spirit-taught words."* The words they spoke on that stage were not words of this world but words that were filled with the wisdom of God. They understood the gift that is Christ our Lord the Holy One.

It was an amazing thing to witness. I assure you that hands were lifted praising the Lord for what he did in them. I could not help but think of what God was doing in the hearts of the teammates that witnessed this. Kam and Xavier encouraged me so much in the Lord and their stories showed me again how God can do amazing things in someone's life. They brought more fire to the fire the Lord had already put in me. Before this point, Kam and Xavier were just teammates that I bonded with through football alone, but now we had an eternal bond in Christ. They soon became my close brothers in Christ that I had a deeper fellowship with. My community just grew again. I say the Lord orchestrated a legendary moment.

Taking Initiative

As a believer in Jesus, you know that urging from the Holy Spirit to step out in faith and do something uncomfortable? Did you find yourself making all the excuses in the book about why you cannot do it? This is exactly what happened to me. Spring of my Junior year the Holy Spirit put it on my heart to start a team bible study. When this was placed on my heart, I made every schedule excuse of why I would not have time. Although, at the end of the day, I could not justify my excuses. So, I decided to hold the bible study for the team, I just had to coordinate the details. I reached out to my teammate Kam and asked him if he wanted to help with the bible study. He thought it was a great idea and we set out to make it happen. After some considerations we decided to hold the bible study at the apartment complex where much of the team stayed. We scheduled to meet once a week in the evening. There were about 7 to 10 guys showing up on average. In that group were all the guys I mentioned in this chapter except Derrick as he had already graduated.

For the studies I printed out sheets that outlined the scriptures we would go over. There was no written method to what we studied but we read whatever the Holy Spirit led us to read. When I first started this group, it was merely out of yielding to the Spirit (which is good) but I did not necessarily want to do it. Although, as the Spirit prevailed, I started enjoying these meetings more. I looked forward to conversing about heavenly things with my teammates. It helped me become even more comfortable sharing about the truth of God's Word. Also, coming to the Father in prayer alongside my teammates was a beautiful thing. I am going to share a scripture that you may have heard before and one that I know I have a thousand times, but it is absolutely true.

Jesus says in Matthew 18:20, *"For where two or three gather in my name, there am I with them."*

I know the Lord used those times to touch everyone's hearts, it most certainly touched mine. Unfortunately, with the onset of Covid we stopped meeting. But that did not stop me, Kam, and others from sharing the Lord and his truth with our teammates. I will share more about that soon.

Pregame Prayer Warrior

Considering praying alongside teammates, I want to share with you about another brother in Christ that the Lord put in my life during my time at OSU. Bradley was a long snapper who was a year ahead of me in school. He transferred in from a team in our conference we played every year. He was a Christ Follower, so when I met him we bonded right away. We regularly attended CrossSports together and connected through conversations of encouragement and edification in the Lord. One day, Bradley came to me and asked me if I wanted to join him in a tradition of his. He asked me if I would join him in praying at the fifteen-yard line before every game. I said of course and obliged to that request. So, before every game Bradley and I ran out to the fifteen-yard line and prayed to the Lord. We expressed our gratitude that he gave us the ability to play the game of football. We asked him for strength, confidence, protection, and that all the glory would be given to him no matter the outcome. Also, every time I prayed, at some point I would say, "Lord guide them hands" because Bradley was a long snapper. That was a prayer I prayed with another long snapper on my team as well. One week Bradley prayed, the next week I prayed, and we alternated like that through the season. Bradley and I became strong brothers in Christ with a deep fellowship anchored in prayer. I believe that when we live out our faith confidently and let our lights shine like Jesus said, we will gravitate towards others who also have that same light. The light of God in me gravitated to the light of God in Bradley. And as the Lord grows our community, we will find ourselves growing as well.

An Unexpected Friendship

For many athletes, the CrossSports ministry was a beacon and highlight of their week. I know it was for me as well. To gather with like-minded athletes and be encouraged by testimonies, conversation, and interaction was a healing thing. It was obvious the group was reserved for OSU athletes only. Although, a guy from California named Jack showed up who did not play sports. He was in the military briefly before enrolling at OSU. When I first met him at CrossSports I thought he was a great guy. Though, I did not think he would become a close brother in Christ as he did. After all, he was not an athlete attending an all-athlete ministry. Like my story with Cormontae, I was mistaken. Each CrossSports meeting we found ourselves increasingly conversing with one another. We exchanged numbers and made time to hang out outside of CrossSports. We also broke bread and attended church together on occasion. He was a guy who always encouraged and prayed for me. His fervent prayer life as a believer challenged me to take praying more seriously. Even to this day we never end our phone calls without praying for each other.

Regarding the CrossSports ministry, Jack and I became emcees for CrossSports, introducing the speakers and closing out the meetings in announcements and prayers. We also both got the opportunity to share our stories and testimonies with the group. One time my senior year I was set to share with the group. Jack was the emcee that night. He said something while introducing me that I will never forget because I have never heard anyone say this before. He said, "My friend and brother is a great man of God and I know he will be an amazing husband one day." When he said that I looked over at him with semi wide eyes. I thought in my head, "hmm, that's new, but I will certainly agree with you in that statement, I know you will be a great husband as well." We often prayed for each other in the arena of relationships and future wives. We both pray that the Lord will help us find a wife that we can serve and love as Christ loved the church and laid down his life for her. I am grateful for my mom in this respect as she is a great example of a godly woman and nurturing mother. We also pray for contentment in our singleness and fellowship with the Lord. We want to become the men that can lead well.

Jack was another brother in Christ that I connected with on that deeper level. I know that the Lord has and will continue to use him in mighty ways even though he is a quote unquote "regular guy." He knows I am kidding; he is far from regular. He is absolutely different, but in a righteous way. I am certainly grateful for his friendship and brotherhood. The Lord answered my prayer again, and my community just got bigger. I know I would not have these brothers if I just prayed and sat at home all day. I had faith the Lord would bless me with meaningful relationships. Being in community was an action that the seed of faith grew into.

Locker Room Witness

In chapter 1, I mentioned that playing football exposed me to people with various kinds of backgrounds and beliefs. The experience of this became more prevalent when I got to college. Players' expressions of their beliefs or "lack thereof" seemed to become more outspoken and opinionated. This was probably because they were older. Although, this did not deter me from what I believed because I knew what I believed was the truth and would believe it if no one else did. Thankfully, I now had brothers to stand firm in that truth with.

In this story, I am particularly talking about myself, Kam, and Xavier. Even though Kam was a newer believer, his knowledge base of God's Word and the wisdom he gained was greater than many "seasoned believers" I knew. It was clear that he not only was filled with the Holy Spirit but was discipled very well by his spiritual leaders. Xavier was the same way, like I said before, they both had a radical shift and were quickly enlightened by the Lord.

As all our lights grew together within the team, many of our teammates were curious about God and his nature.

Some questioned the reliability of the Bible. Others could not accept a God who sent people to hell. This inspired me to go deep into Christian Apologetics. Christian Apologetics is the practice of defending the faith with logic, reason, and evidence. Much of my studies of apologetics occurred during the Covid lockdown. I remember watching men like Frank Turek, William Lane Craig, and J. Warner Wallace. They answered many of the pressing questions people had about God and Christianity. For example, why does God allow evil things to happen? Who created God? Is not the Bible and the gospels of Matthew, Mark, Luke, and John unreliable and tampered with? Didn't the gospel writers fabricate a story about Christ that is not true?

These were some of the questions our teammates had. There were times that Kam, Xavier, and I all sat with our teammates for hours listening to their concerns and answering questions about God and the Bible the best way we knew how. Sometimes I had to go to class, but the conversation was so good that I did not want to leave. Some of our teammates were receptive to the truth. Others were still on the fence. And still others just wanted to debate. Nonetheless, it was great sharpening and training for us to always be ready to share what we believed. Not just that "we grew up with it." I know you remember that from earlier, that will not work in these situations. In 1 Peter 3:15 it writes, *"But in your hearts revere Christ as Lord. Always be prepared to give an answer to everyone who asks you to give the reason for the hope that you have. But do this with gentleness and respect."* This is what we are challenged to do as believers.

We must be confident in what we believe, know that it is true, and be ready to share it at any moment. Being on the OSU football team was a great arena to practice this.

We desired for the light of God to shine in a dark world. Especially in a dark locker room. Anyone that has played football or other sports before knows what kind of dirty talk goes down in the locker room. We kicked a lot of darkness out that otherwise would have been there had we not been salt and light and brought holy flavor to that place. I was profoundly grateful to have brothers that I could shine brighter with than I ever could alone. I never imagined these kinds of conversations would take place when I went to Ohio State.

I want to mention that as believers in Christ, we do not save anyone but only the gospel has the power to save. Romans 1:16 says, *"For I am not ashamed of the gospel, because it is the power of God that brings salvation to every-one who believes: first to the Jew, then to the Gentile."* Even though Kam, Xavier, and I did our best to defend the faith and answer many objections, the greatest thing we shared with our teammates was the gospel of Jesus Christ. The Holy Spirit helped us plant seeds of truth in people that I pray God grows one day, because only he can make it grow.

"Stage Fright"

Sometimes we allow "stage fright" to deter us from sharing the truth of the gospel with others. When I say stage fright, I mean being afraid to talk with people about our faith, rather it is one person or a group of people. This in fact is a selfish thing to do. Most of us are simply more afraid of what others will think than we are bold about the truth of the gospel that can save someone's life. If there was a person about to be flattened by a train, we would not be worried about what they thought when we pleaded with them to get off the track, would we? No, we would not. This is because we know telling them the truth about the situation is more important than what they think about us. In other words, the lives of people are more valuable than our insecurities. Ask the Lord for boldness and the Holy Spirit to give you the words to say when the time is right. Understand that when I say this, I am not just talking to you as the reader, but also myself. We can do it. Amen?

Jesus Calls us to...

Jesus calls his followers to be servants as he was. In fact, when we serve others, it not only blesses those we serve, but it makes us great. It makes us great because we obey the Lord, and when we obey the Lord, favor and reward tend to follow. In the next chapter let us look at how my community and I served others needs and how it blessed us. Be inspired!

SERVE AND BE GREAT!

²⁵Jesus called them together and said, "You know that the rulers of the Gentiles lord it over them, and their high officials exercise authority over them. ²⁶Not so with you. Instead, whoever wants to become great among you must be your servant, ²⁷and whoever wants to be first must be your slave— ²⁸just as the Son of Man did not come to be served, but to serve, and to give his life as a ransom for many."
- Matthew 20:25-28

Inspired to Serve

Has there ever been someone in your life that was a giver? Someone that intentionally searched for ways they could bless someone else's life. Someone that never asked for anything but gave everything? In my life, this was a picture of Bob and Elaine. They wanted to serve everyone they came across. My family and I certainly were grateful for the way they served us. I mentioned previously that the doors of their home were always open to us. Even when they were not in town, they welcomed my family to stay at their place when they came to watch my games. They always invited me to their family events and gatherings. Making great food to satisfy our stomachs and showering everyone with love was a normal occurrence. They not only served their family well but served their community well.

Bob and Elaine lived on a farm that had several acres of land. Instead of using the harvest of that land for monetary gain, they gave it away. They grew corn every year and when the time was right, they freely gave all that corn to the people at the church, in the community, and other places that needed it.

They also served food at a ministry Resource Center in Columbus called Jordan's Crossing. Jordan's Crossing provided food, clothes, addiction treatment, job referrals, and shower and laundry services, among other things for those in need. With their own hands, Bob and Elaine made hundreds of meals a week for the center and those same hands distributed many of those meals. They not only fed food to satisfy the physical hunger of those in need but also fed them the truth of Christ that satisfies all spiritual hunger and provides our every need. In chapter three I talked about Matthew twenty where Jesus shared with his disciples that if they want to be considered great, they must do as he did and live a life of service. Bob and Elaine's example encouraged me to be more like Jesus.

I decided to serve at Jordan's Crossing with them in the offseason. Bob and Elaine would cook, and I helped pass out the food to those that came. Handing out food and saying a quick "enjoy and God bless you" was enough to put a smile on their faces. I also spoke with some of the individuals and empathized with their circumstances, encouraged them in the Lord, and prayed for them. I enjoyed going and serving at Jordan's Crossing so much that I invited my whole running back group to serve as well. I also invited my pregame prayer warrior Bradley. If you do not already know, literally everyone in Ohio is a diehard Ohio State Buckeye fan. So, when they saw all of us, it brought joy to them. It was important to show them that they were valuable and worth our time. We all enjoyed serving as it gave us joy to give out joy. I not only gave my time and efforts to serve Jordan's Crossing, but I also gave my platform as I shared their mission and ministry on my social media.

This reminds me of a passage of scripture. James 1:9-10 says, *"Believers in humble circumstances ought to take pride in their high position. But the rich should take pride in their humiliation—since they will pass away like a wildflower."* This verse addresses the perspectives that believers in Christ should take depending on what circumstance of life they are in. If you are a poor believer, you should boast and rejoice in the riches you have in Christ and eternity because those are the riches that truly matter. On the other hand, if you are a rich believer, you should take a humble position understanding that riches do not make you more valuable than others because they will all pass away one day. Rather, rejoice in the great riches you have freely been given in Christ and eternity. When we serve those believers in poorer circumstances than ourselves, we remind them that they are rich in Christ. We show them that our wealth does not make us more valuable than they are, but it is there for us to serve those in need in a humble fashion.

To The Streets

The best way to do ourselves good is to be doing good to others; the best way to gather is to scatter.
- Thomas Brooks

Since I already served at Jordan's Crossing helping the needy, I decided to take it a step further, so I went to the streets. On campus there was a street that led straight into downtown Columbus. I often saw homeless people on the sidewalk just laying down or asking for help. Those of you that know Columbus probably know the street that I am talking about. On weekend evenings I often drove down that road and stopped to help them. This was a time when most people went out to the bars and got ready for a night of partying or hanging out with friends. Many of them walked right past these folks without a glance. While everyone was getting ready to indulge and satisfy themselves, I was ready to satisfy someone else. I asked those laying on the sidewalk or holding signs asking for help if they were hungry. If they wanted, I bought them some food and then lent my ear to them. Many of them would really open up about their situation and deep wounds in their lives. I wanted to listen to them in their situation. No mention of me being an OSU football player, just someone who wanted to serve another. There were some people that I helped several times. It was like starting off where we left off. After listening, I shared the hope of Christ and prayed with them. I also made sure to put some extra socks and a few clothes in my car that I no longer wore just in case someone needed some extra warmth in the cold winters.

Like most things, I do not know how the Lord used those encounters for his glory and moving the hearts of people. All we can do is show and share the love and truth of Christ. Proverbs 19:17 says, *"Whoever is kind to the poor lends to the Lord, and he will reward them for what they have done."* We as believers must realize that while we were spiritually poor and dead, Christ loved us and laid down his life so we could become rich. We know that Christ gave us everything even though we had nothing to offer him. Out of his pure holiness and goodness he provides for our needs irrespective of what we do. He is faithful because he is faithful and nothing else. We of course cannot save anyone, but we ought to give people a glimpse into this great love we received by the way we love others. We should lend a hand to those in need out of the pure holiness and goodness we have been given. We do this without expecting anything in return from that person. In fact, according to that proverb, we have a better return from the Lord than anything that a person could give us. To fill someone else's cup is to be filled up yourself. I understand this is a hard concept to grasp. We all are naturally selfish and looking out for ourselves often times seems like the best path to joy, peace, and purpose. It is in fact the opposite. I pray we all come to that realization and be moved to serve others more.

Athletes Feeding Appetites

Considering feeding the needy, we were inspired to do this through the CrossSports ministry as well. Tom, Julie, and some others got together some food bags with water for the athletes to pass out. We took these bags and went in groups of five to ten walking downtown Columbus searching for people to bless with some food, conversation, prayer, and encouragement in their circumstance. We would approach a person and say, "Excuse me, we would like to bless you with some food if you are hungry." Most would accept with a thank you. Others accepted with no reaction or words. We asked them what their names were and talked with them however much or little they wanted. Again, we wanted to lend an ear and show we cared. We then made a request saying, "could my friends and I pray for you?" I do not think one person declined that invitation. All of us would circle up and cover that person in prayer and shower them with the love of God. We were out for a few hours blessing and praying for people. It was a real joy to do this with fellow believers and fellow athletes. It is again a reminder that we are blessed to bless others.

It is like a river flowing as it both gives and receives. The reasons rivers flow is because they have an abundance of water that they cannot hold on their own. So, they distribute that water to other areas allowing the land, the animals, and people to flourish. We as believers are over-flowing with blessings so we can pour out that blessing on others. When we give blessings, we receive blessings. The more blessings we give, the more blessings we receive, so we can bless even more.

In John 10:10 Jesus says, *"The thief comes only to steal and kill and destroy. I came that they may have life and have it abundantly."*

So, this thief (the corrupt religious leaders in biblical context), do the opposite of our Lord which is steal, kill, and destroy. Since Jesus has given us life abundantly, it should overflow to others so they can get a taste of that life. So, instead of stealing, killing, and destroying, we can give, bring life, and restore the people we come in contact with. Amen?

A Night to Shine

As serving is a theme in this chapter, I want to share about another time that several of my teammates and I did just that. In 2020, my junior year, Rock City Church hosted an event called Night To Shine. Night To Shine is an event created by Tim Tebow's Foundation that gives special needs age 14 and older the chance to experience a prom night. We were told about this event through our team player personnel staff. This was an event that myself and about 10 other teammates volunteered for. Rock City also hosted this event in 2019 and many of my teammates and I went then as well. This event was a chance for us to show all special needs that they are important, precious, valued, and loved by God.

I was what was called a "buddy" my first-year volunteering for the event in 2019. A buddy would be a prom date for a special need individual attending the event. So, I was a buddy to a young lady named Colleen who was deaf and autistic, and she used American Sign Language (ASL). For me to communicate with her I had to learn some signs. Colleen had a translator with her, so she helped me learn a few words and phrases. One of the phrases I learned was "you look beautiful." So much of the night I would sign to her and remind her that she in fact looked beautiful. I crowned her prom queen of the night, we danced, and took pictures together. I believe Colleen really had a great time being celebrated and loved on. I was most certainly blessed to be her buddy and celebrate all the special needs there. Colleen inspired me to take ASL class in school. I am certainly not fluid, but I still know a few signs and occasionally refresh myself on some of them. When the event was over, I said farewell to Colleen, and I figured that would be the last time I would see her. The crazy thing is that the next year I volunteered and guess what, I was Colleen's date again! It was like we were destined to be together. It was a heartwarming thing to see her a year later and remind her that she looked beautiful.

My teammates were also buddies of other special needs and I know they have their own stories of how it blessed them to make their dates feel special. We all left that event with smiles on our faces as we were filled with joy because we gave someone else joy. We were profoundly blessed to serve the special needs in our community and created a memory we will never forget.

Still More...

The collection of stories that I shared thus far are not the only ones that God used to shine his light and plant seeds (God is still using athletes and students at OSU to shine his light today). There were other acts of service and outreach that I and other brothers and sisters in Christ were blessed to do. I also made great relationships with other brothers in Christ as well. Although, I do not want to bombard anyone with story after story. I just want to show you that as a follower of Christ, you can flourish in college, or wherever you go, or wherever you are. You can impact others for the Kingdom of God. And being in community will give you more strength to do that than being alone ever could. So, get in community!

DO IT TO "THE LEAST OF THESE"

Are You a Sheep?

Jesus establishes two categories of people, the sheep, and the goats. He outlines the difference of these two while on the Mount of Olives in a sermon that was one of many he preached. These collections of sermons were answers to his disciples asking about the end times and Jesus's second coming on the earth. In Matthew 24:3 they asked Jesus, *"Tell us," they said, "when will this happen, and what will be the sign of your coming and of the end of the age?"* Let's focus on the last answer that Jesus gave them in Matthew 25 where he distinguishes between his sheep (Christ Followers) and the goats (non-believers) and how Jesus will reward and punish them. Let's look at the sheep.

In Matthew 25:31-40 it writes, *"When the Son of Man comes in his glory, and all the angels with him, he will sit on his glorious throne. All the nations will be gathered before him, and he will separate the people one from another as a shepherd separates the sheep from the goats. He will put the sheep on his right and the goats on his left. "Then the King will say to those on his right, 'Come, you who are blessed by my Father; take your inheritance, the kingdom prepared for you since the creation of the world. For I was hungry and you gave me something to eat, I was thirsty and you gave me something to drink, I was a stranger and you invited me in, I needed clothes and you clothed me, I was sick and you looked after me, I was in prison and you came to visit me.' "Then the righteous will answer him, 'Lord, when did we see you hungry and feed you, or thirsty and give you something to drink? When did we see you a stranger and invite you in, or needing clothes and clothe you? When did we see you sick or in prison and go to visit you?' "The King will reply, 'Truly I tell you, whatever you did for one of the least of these brothers and sisters of mine, you did for me."*

So, here is Jesus describing the believer. We are known as children of God by the way we love others. The "least of these" are those who are in needy situations, especially other believers. Notice how Jesus says when we do good by the "least of these" we do good by him. Isn't it ironic that when we do good by the "least of these" we are simultaneously doing good by the "greatest of these" which is Jesus who now sits on the thrown with a name above every name. These acts of love through serving the "least of these" is the action that flows out of the abundance of our salvation. Notice I said it flows out of our salvation and is not required for our salvation. We are not saved by these good works of love, but we sure display them once we are saved through Christ. These works come from a right relationship with God so that these deeds are done for the kingdom of God for his glory and not for the kingdom of self for our glory. This makes us blessed by the Creator (our Father) and yields us an eternal inheritance and "the kingdom prepared for us since the creation of the world." Wow, how beautiful that is. This is contrary to that of the goat (non-believer), let's look at how Jesus describes them.

Are you a Goat?

In Matthew 25:41-46 it writes, *"Then he will say to those on his left, 'Depart from me, you who are cursed, into the eternal fire prepared for the devil and his angels. For I was hungry and you gave me nothing to eat, I was thirsty and you gave me nothing to drink, I was a stranger and you did not invite me in, I needed clothes and you did not clothe me, I was sick and in prison and you did not look after me.' "They also will answer, 'Lord, when did we see you hungry or thirsty or a stranger or needing clothes or sick or in prison, and did not help you?' "He will reply, 'Truly I tell you, whatever you did not do for one of the least of these, you did not do for me.' "Then they will go away to eternal punishment, but the righteous to eternal life."*

This is the lot of the goat (unbeliever). Goats cannot do good to the "least of these" the way God desires because they are not a part of his kingdom, but the kingdom of darkness. And darkness has nothing to do with light. Although, we who are a part of the kingdom of God (sheep) are full of light. God leverages that light for his glory and the prosperity of those that light touches on both ends of receiving and giving. This is why we can do the good to the "least of these" that God desires. We are in a win win situation when we shine the light of God by doing good, serving, and loving others. The only outcome is greatness. So, are you a sheep or a goat?

In the last chapter we are going to discuss more about what it means and looks like to be great, act on our faith, and be in community for our flourishing.

EMPOWERED FOR MORE

"Good works do not make a good man, but a good man does good works."
- Martin Luther

SPURRING YOU ON...

Why Serving Makes Us Great

When we think of Jesus, why is he the greatest figure in history (no debate)? Well, it is because he impacted and served people beyond measure. In fact, he only thought of the good of others his whole life. He did not commit one selfish, greedy, envious, or prideful act. The result of that was that he was given a name above every name that every knee will inevitably bow to, and every tongue will inevitably confess to. There is a passage of scripture that will help us see how we as believers are to adopt this same mindset for greatness.

Philippians 2:5-11 says, *"In your relationships with one another, have the same mindset as Christ Jesus: Who, being in very nature God, did not consider equality with God something to be used to his own advantage; rather, he made himself nothing by taking the very nature of a servant, being made in human likeness. And being found in appearance as a man, he humbled himself by becoming obedient to death— even death on a cross! Therefore God exalted him to the highest place and gave him the name that is above every name, that at the name of Jesus every knee should bow, in heaven and on earth and under the earth, and every tongue acknowledge that Jesus Christ is Lord, to the glory of God the Father."*

Jesus displayed humbleness through servanthood. That servanthood was so great that it yielded both Jesus and us the highest most glorious reward. Jesus got a name above every name that even those who reject him will have no choice but to bow and confess that he is Lord. We got the gift of restored fellowship and eternal security with the Father. You see how Jesus's humbleness and act of self-lessness did not leave him empty handed but rewarded both him and those he served. This is why we are blessed to be a blessing. When we serve, we not only gift someone else, but the byproduct of that service is a gift for our-selves. I am not suggesting we should serve for a reward, but we should know that we are rewarded through service. Those are two different things. I am also not saying that we will gain rewards by the world's standard as that is not guaranteed. I am most certainly saying that our reward is sure in eternity, our riches are guaranteed there (we talked some about that reward in the last chapter). Our heart for service should purely come from a place of obedience and love for God and love for others as ourselves. Jesus is our ultimate example for this, so be like Jesus. This is how we become great.

Faith in Action

Let us now look at these Philippians 2 verses in another way. Let us look at it in four parts. The four parts are mind-set, humbleness, obedience, and reward. Before we can be humble and obey the Father (God) the way Jesus did, we have to obtain the right mindset. That mindset is a mind set on God and not self. When our mind is set on God, we then can humble ourselves under his authority and obey his command. When we humble ourselves under his authority and obey his command, reward follows. Reward follows because you sowed a seed that God produced, and that seed only creates life. This is true in our salvation as well. When we sow a seed of faith in Christ, that seed was provided by God, and it created in us a new person that passed from death to life. This is also true after we received salvation. When we sow a seed of obedience, God gave us the power to obey, and it creates in us good deeds. These good deeds are from God, and they can never produce a negative result in God's kingdom. These good deeds are never selfish and always serves and does good for others according to what God says is good for them. Any other kind of deed will not serve in God's kingdom and therefore is not a good one.

Doing good deeds that come from a mind set on God and humbleness and obedience to his authority is what allows us to let his Kingdom come and his will be done on earth as it is in heaven. This is why the scripture says in Hebrews 10:24-25, *"And let us consider how we may spur one another on toward love and good deeds, not giving up meeting to- gether, as some are in the habit of doing, but encouraging one another—and all the more as you see the Day approach- ing."* This is what I am trying to do right now, spur you onto good deeds through this book and not mediocre Christian- ity void of substance. We are not saved by good deeds, but they are the substance (byproduct) of our faith in Christ. Faith does not exist without action, they co-exist.

Keep Community

So, in regard to community, let us look at Hebrews 10:24-25 again. It says, *"And let us consider how we may spur one another on toward love and good deeds, not giving up meeting together, as some are in the habit of doing, but encouraging one another—and all the more as you see the Day approaching."* Are we as followers of Christ looking for ways to encourage other believers to be a light in this dark world? Or are we just going along with the flow of chaos? I think the reason many of us do not encourage others to be light is because we are not being a light ourselves. So of course, we cannot tell someone to be something that we are not. That would be hypocritical. This is why these verses use words like *"let us"* and *"one another"* and *"meeting together."* This is a community kind of thing. When we are in community with other believers, we will be spurred on to do these great deeds that we discussed throughout this book and more. These deeds are evidence that the faith we proclaim in Christ is real.

Now what does verse 25 mean more in depth? It says this, *"not giving up meeting together, as some are in the habit of doing, but encouraging one another—and all the more as you see the Day approaching."* Let us zoom in on *"the Day approaching."* What is this day?

Revelation 22:12 says, *"Look, I am coming soon! My reward is with me, and I will give to each person according to what they have done."*

Have you ever had someone in your life that you dearly loved because you saw the great sacrifices they made for your well-being? Did you feel like you wanted to make them proud because of all the things they did for you? Did their love push you to strive for excellence in life? I know this is the case for many people out there. Well, how much more should we do this on account of Jesus and what he did for us? In 2 Corinthians 5:20-21 it says, *"We are therefore Christ's ambassadors, as though God were making his appeal through us. We implore you on Christ's behalf: Be reconciled to God. God made him who had no sin to be sin for us, so that in him we might become the righteousness of God."*

We are to show Jesus off and represent him in the world like an ambassador of a country shows off and represents their country in loyalty and honor. Jesus is returning soon for his church (the body of Christ), and we will want to have done good with the gift we have been given. That gift is faith and salvation in Christ Jesus our Lord. What did we do with that gift? Did we bury it? Or were we unashamed of it, living it out, and expressing the truth of Christ through love and good deeds to shine our light in a dark world? So do not neglect fellowship and community with believers. This is how we encourage one another to be unashamed and be the light that leads others to the source of light. Rest assured that darkness has no space when our light shines in this place. Let's do it together!

So, with all that I finally say this: Be encouraged and inspired to be in community, be the light God calls you to be, and make Kingdom impact. God bless you and Shalom.

BUILDING COMMUNITY
RESOURCES

RESOURCES FOR COLLEGE STUDENTS

Every Student Sent

https://everystudentsent.org/

Christian Care Box

https://www.christiancarebox.com/

Set Apart Girl

https://setapart.org/

Intervarsity

https://intervarsity.org/

Barna Group (Article)

https://www.barna.com/research/resilient-
disciples/

BIBLICAL REFERENCES

SCRIPTURAL REFERENCES

CHAPTER 2

JOSHUA 1:8

PSALM 19:1-2

MATTHEW 7:13-14

COLOSSIANS 3:23

MATTHEW 22:37-39

CORINTHIANS 12:9

COLOSSIANS 3:16

MATTHEW 5:16

1 TIMOTHY 4:12

CHAPTER 3

1 CORINTHIANS 3:11

ISAIAH 64:6

EPHESIANS 2:8

PROVERBS 27:17

HEBREWS 10:24-25

PROVERBS 24:9

EPHESIANS 6:12

EPHESIANS 6:13-17

1 PETER 5:8

CHAPTER 4

JOHN 15:5

GENESIS 2:15

GENESIS 1:28

1 PETER 3:15

PROVERBS 13:20

MATTHEW 20:25-28

PROVERBS 24:6

GENESIS 3:4-6

JOHN 2:16

ECCLESIASTES 4:9-10

PSALMS 145:17-18

PHILIPPIANS 4:6-7

CHAPTER 5

NUMBERS 18

2 CHRONICLES 13

MATTHEW 5:14-16

GENESIS 1:16

MATTHEW 2:9-11

PROVERBS 9:10

1 CORINTHIANS 2:11-13

MATTHEW 18:20

1 PETER 3:15

ROMANS 1:16

CHAPTER 6

MATTHEW 20:25-28

JAMES 1:9-10

PROVERBS 19:17

JOHN 10:10

MATTHEW 24:3

MATTHEW 25:31-40

MATTHEW 25:41-46

CHAPTER 7

PHILIPPIANS 2:5-11

HEBREWS 10:24-25

REVELATION 22:12

2 CORINTHIANS 5:20-21

Master Teague III is a Christ Follower hailing from Murfreesboro Tennessee. He is an alumnus of The Ohio State University
and played running back for the buckeyes from 2018-2021.

Visit masterwteagueiii.com learn more.